Cognitive-Behavioral Therapy

CBT Skills
Workbook

Practical Exercises and Worksheets to Promote Change

Dr. Barry M. Gregory

Published by:

PESI, LLC
PO Box 1000
3839 White Avenue
Eau Claire, Wisconsin 54702

Printed in the United States of America

ISBN: 978-1-936128-02-0

Disclaimer and Author's Copyright Policy

This workbook includes exercises and worksheets to help people learn new skills, but is not a substitute for professional diagnosis and treatment for mental health disorders. For those who use the book on their own they do so at their own risk and are advised to contact a mental health professional if they experience any mental health difficulties, if they are having suicidal thoughts, or have a plan. Suicidal clients are advised to call 911 immediately if they are having an emergency and/or to speak with a mental health professional.

While every effort has been made to assure that the information in the workbook is accurate and reflects current evidence-based practices in the mental health field, no guarantee can be given that the workbook is completely free from error or omission. The worksheets and the exercises reflect the author's philosophy and creative application of cognitive-behavioral theories and therapies. The reference section cites and acknowledges the pioneers and creators of CBT and the many excellent sources that were used to create this workbook.

Finally, all information in the *CBT Skills Workbook* is protected by copyright. Professionals who purchase the workbook are granted permission to use any and all of the worksheets in their professional practice with their clients which includes photocopy privileges. Permission to photocopy the entire workbook is not granted and is considered a violation of the copyright policy. Any questions about appropriate use of the workbook in groups or research should be directed to the author. No information in this workbook can be published or reproduced without the expressed written consent of the author.

Premier Education Solutions strives to obtain knowledgeable authors and faculty for its publications and seminars. The clinical recommendations contained herein are the result of extensive author research and review. Obviously, any recommendations for patient care must be held up against individual circumstances currently accepted practice. However, these recommendations cannot be considered universal and complete. The authors and publisher repudiate any responsibility for unfavorable effects that result from information, recommendations, undetected omissions or errors. Professionals using this publication should research other original sources of authority as well.

For information on this and other Premier Education Solutions manuals
and audio recordings, please call 800-844-8260 or visit our website at www.pesi.com

www.pesi.com

About the Author

Dr. Barry M. Gregory, Ed.D., M.Ed., LMHC, NCC is the President of the National Addictions Treatment Institute and adjunct professor at Barry University. He maintains a professional training, consultation and counseling practice in Boynton Beach, Fl. He has a Doctor of Education degree with a major in Educational Leadership and a Master of Education degree with a major in counselor education from Florida Atlantic University. He completed his BA degree in Psychology at Johnson State College. Barry is a State of Florida Licensed Mental Health Counselor and a National Certified Counselor. The National Addictions Treatment Institute is an approved provider of continuing education seminars by the Florida Certification Board. He is also a member of the American Psychological Association.

His doctoral dissertation (Gregory, 2001) was one of the first published studies on the efficacy of using brief motivational and skill-building interventions with intercollegiate student athletes to help reduce high-risk drinking. He has presented his research findings at national conferences, served as a faculty member at several colleges and universities and as an assistant director of a university counseling center. Dr. Gregory has consulted with colleges and universities on research with high-risk drinking, published white papers on college binge drinking, authored the College Success Workbook, served as a mobile assessor in the Access to Recovery federal grant for the homeless, and served on state and local substance abuse prevention community coalitions. He currently collaborates to write grants and serves as a grant evaluator for local, state and federal grants including a criminal justice family drug court to help abused and neglected children with addicted parents.

Dr. Gregory is well-known for his warm, personal and nonjudgmental approach to helping people find solutions for their most challenging problems. With over 15 years of direct clinical experiences with diverse populations, he has expertise with practical hands-on CBT strategies that work. His expertise in motivational strategies and cognitive-behavioral therapy approaches come not only from his formal education, training, and supervision, but from his extensive clinical experiences with clients. This blending of research and practice is reflected in the publication of this new CBT skills workbook.

With a passion for teaching and learning, Dr. Gregory has developed a career of providing national training seminars for mental health professionals across the United States. He has developed and provided over 500 training seminars on evidence-based practices including motivational interviewing, cognitive-behavioral therapy, suicide, ethics, depression and bipolar disorder, alcohol and other drug addictions, high-risk college drinking, CBT, PTSD and Trauma, and co-occurring disorders. Dr. Gregory is well-known for his fun, interactive and information seminars.

Again, his focus on what works is evident at his training seminars where participants continue to say they like the hands-on practical take-home and use the next day tools for the toolbox approach. The CBT workbook features practical tools for the toolbox.

Dr. Gregory has also appeared on local health-focused radio programs and MSNBC for a one-hour documentary on college binge drinking entitled *Party 101* and has developed a website designed to provide consumers and professionals with easy access to information and resources on addictions and mental health. He is an active member of the American Psychological Association and volunteers as a member of the Palm Beach County Substance Abuse Coalition. He will personally respond to any questions people have about the workbook and contact information is provided.

Dr. Barry M. Gregory
National Addictions Treatment Institute
8934 Via Tuscany Dr.
Boynton Beach, FL 33472
http://natiwebsite.com
drbarrygregory@comcast.net

Cognitive-Behavioral Therapy

Cognitive-Behavioral Therapy (CBT) is one of the fastest-growing psychotherapies in the world, largely because it has been clinically tested and found effective for a broad-range of psychiatric, psychological, and mental health problems. Over 400 published empirical studies reviewing the literature on treatment outcomes have consistently demonstrated that CBT is effective in treating depression, general anxiety disorder, panic disorder, social phobia, posttraumatic stress disorder, childhood depressive and anxiety disorders, marital distress, anger, childhood somatic disorders, chronic pain, obsessive-compulsive disorders, bulimia nervosa, and schizophrenia (Butler, A.C., Chapman, J.E., Forman, E.M., & Beck, A. T. 2006). CBT also has strong clinical support from both clients and professionals who like its collaborative process and practical tools and strategies for solving everyday problems.

CBT is an umbrella term combining many traditional and innovative cognitive and behavioral theories and therapies. It has a rich collection of proven techniques designed to help people challenge negative thoughts, learn positive new behaviors, prevent relapse, set goals, regulate emotions, dispute irrational beliefs, and solve problems. CBT interventions help people navigate tough challenges and build happier, more meaningful lives. Newer approaches help people learn to become more mindful of the present moment and more accepting of unpleasant situations, thoughts, feelings, and behaviors. Together CBT provides mental health professionals with a wealth of practical tools and techniques for their toolbox.

Cognitive Therapy

Central to CBT is the role thoughts, feelings, and behaviors play in the development and maintenance of family, health, relationship, and mental health problems. Perceptions of daily events and past memories can strongly influence feelings and behaviors. Helping people become more aware of how everyday situations can trigger automatic thoughts, strong emotional feelings and behaviors is key in cognitive therapy. By examining the accuracy of thoughts and beliefs, mental health professionals can help clients develop more realistic and balanced ways of thinking, feeling, and acting.

To illustrate how thoughts trigger feelings and behaviors, imagine getting stuck in bumper to bumper traffic on a major highway in a large city. People stuck in traffic may think: (1) this situation is awful, (2) it's not fair, (3) why me, (4) other drivers are idiots, and/or (5) bad things only happen to me. These automatic thoughts can make people feel anxious, irritated, frustrated, or annoyed. These negative emotions can trigger relief seeking behaviors like screaming, pointing, yelling, tailgating, or gesturing. Helping people become aware of the relationship between everyday situations, thoughts, feelings, behaviors, and the body is one of the most important skills to learn in CBT.

Counselors and therapists can help clients learn to identify, evaluate, and modify their distorted thinking patterns or faulty beliefs. Like thought detectives, they can help clients look for the *evidence* that supports or does not support their thoughts. Like lawyers, they can help clients to question negative thoughts by reviewing the facts and evidence. Cognitive therapy helps people identify, evaluate, and modify thoughts and beliefs. Realistic and balanced thinking is key in CBT.

According to Dr. Aaron T. Beck, founder of Cognitive Therapy, depressed clients learn and develop automatic negative thoughts and core beliefs about self, others, and the world. Clinicians can help clients discover that these *thoughts are not facts* even though they may feel and act like they are true. Deeper maladaptive beliefs learned from childhood are at the root of many underlying repetitive presenting and behavioral problems.

Setting goals, forming a good therapeutic alliance, and helping people modify their core beliefs are some of the most effective strategies in treating Axis II personality disorders (Beck, Freeman, & Davis, 2004).

Dr. Beck also identified cognitive distortions or thinking errors in the way people process information. When people are upset, these feelings are often preceded by a series of automatic thoughts or self-statements. People develop mental habits like filtering information where the brain tends to focus only on the negative. Helping people identify and label distortions can help people learn how to develop more balanced and positive thinking habits.

Rational Emotive Behavioral Therapy

In Dr. Albert Ellis's Rational Emotive Behavioral Therapy (REBT), therapists actively teach clients the ABC technique. This technique is designed to help people learn how to challenge irrational beliefs and replace them with more rational ones. According to Dr. Ellis, it's not what happens, it's what people say or tell themselves about what happens. Helping people develop rational beliefs, flexible preferences, frustration tolerance, and unconditional self-acceptance are key in REBT.

Behavioral Therapies

In addition to cognitive therapy techniques, CBT has a rich tradition of behavioral therapies where the principles of learning are used to help people change self-defeating behaviors. Behavioral approaches have been strongly influenced by the work of Pavlov's classic conditioning, Wolfe's systematic desensitization, Skinner's operant conditioning, and Bandera's social learning theory. To help people change or modify a behavior, behaviorists use reinforcement, consequences, and shaping (Leonard, Follette & Compton, 2006). Setting goals and measuring progress are key strategies in behavioral therapies. Positive reinforcement is much more effective than punishment is shaping positive new behaviors.

New Behavior Therapies include Dialectical Behavioral Therapy (DBT), Behavioral Activation, and Acceptance and Commitment Therapy (ACT). In DBT, people learn mindfulness, interpersonal effectiveness, emotion regulation, and distress tolerance skills; in Behavioral Activation, depressed people learn that activation is key to improving mood; and in Acceptance and Commitment Therapy people learn how to accept the things they can't change and make a commitment to a course of action that reflects their most cherished values.

Top behavioral therapy intervention techniques include: modeling, relaxation training and breathing techniques, systematic desensitization, exposure therapies, assertiveness training, graded task assignment, increasing pleasurable activities, self-esteem training, problem-solving, moderation management skills, self-monitoring techniques, activity scheduling, contingency management techniques, relapse prevention, and coping skills training. Positive action plans with goals and action steps are key to helping people initiate and maintain lasting behavioral change. To learn new behavioral habits or new skills takes repeated practice, role play and rehearsal. Practicing small steps over and over again increases self-efficacy and the new habit becomes wired in the brain. We can train our brain to think, feel, and act differently with repeated practice.

Feeling Better Strategies

CBT can also help people learn how to regulate emotions and manage their feelings. Clients are sometimes overwhelmed by the unexpected tidal waves of emotional pain. Intense emotional reactions often motivate people to engage in self-defeating, relief-seeking behaviors like avoidance, substance abuse, or suicidal behaviors. CBT helps people become more aware of their feelings and how to identify situations that trigger these feelings. Emotional regulation skills, or feeling better strategies, help clients cope with the challenges of everyday life.

CBT and Brain-Based Strategies

Contemporary CBT combines and integrates evidence-based practices from a wide range of approaches including the mind-body connection. Brain-based research is charting new territory for mental health professionals to use brain-friendly strategies in everyday clinical practice. CBT can help to wire and fire new neurological activity in the brain and help people change the meaning of traumatic memories (Cozolino, 2002). With hard work and repeated practice new thoughts, feelings, and behaviors can become wired in the brain. Research confirms that the brain continues to heal, grow and develop throughout the life span. Helping people learn more about the brain can help them to learn more effective ways to change thoughts, feelings, and behaviors (Begley, 2008; Amen, 1998).

CBT and the Environment

The environment and relationships also have a significant impact on peoples' thoughts, feelings and behaviors. Improving interpersonal skills can radically improve mood by teaching clients how to cope with dysfunctional family communication patterns and interactions. Family-based interventions help to address some of the potential root causes that exacerbate and maintain a client's self-destructive patterns. Mental health professionals are challenged to help people learn how to cope with the impact that the environment has on their problems. Relapse is often triggered by high-risk situations and environments that perpetuate self-defeating behaviors. While unaddressed environmental and relationship influences pose significant challenges for both clients and clinicians, advances in CBT integrate strategies that help clients learn to navigate both environmental, family and other relationship challenges. The therapeutic relationship is the ideal place to help people have more effective interpersonal skills.

CBT and the Body

Finally, CBT is increasingly recognizing the way events, experiences, thoughts, feelings and behaviors trigger physical reactions in the body. Significant events like trauma, depression, anger and anxiety produce physical reactions in the body. Some people are better at sensing with their body and benefit more from body-based therapies. Paying attention to body language, facial expression, and tone of voice are important for mental health professionals. Suggesting physical exercise and increased activity can have amazing psychological and physical results for the client.

CBT in Nutshell

In short, CBT can help people develop new coping skills, improve relationships, overcome fears, improve mindfulness skills, develop greater acceptance, challenge irrational beliefs, and build happier, more meaningful lives. CBT is a collaborative therapy designed to help clients explore options, set goals, and solve problems. While not a magic bullet, CBT provides hope everyday to people facing some of life's toughest challenges. Contemporary CBT attempts to integrate techniques from a broad spectrum of therapies and it's continued success is largely due to the ongoing research that continues to demonstrate that it works for a broad range of psychological problems. Today, motivational, cognitive, and behavioral interventions are combined to provide highly-effective treatments for a broad spectrum of mental health problems.

How to Use the CBT Skills Workbook

Using the CBT Skills Workbook

Advances in evidence-based practices like CBT have increased the need for mental health professionals to advance their skills and competencies in these best practices. The challenge for many clinicians is finding practical ways to integrate empirically-supported therapies into everyday clinical practice. While there are many excellent books on the theory and practice of cognitive-behavioral therapies, this workbook provides powerful and practical worksheets and exercises to help clinicians integrate CBT tools and techniques into everyday practice.

The purpose of the workbook is to help clinicians help individuals and families learn CBT skills to facilitate change and improve the quality of their lives. CBT skills will empower and motivate people to learn how to modify automatic negative thinking habits, painful emotional reactions, and self-defeating behavior patterns. While learning new skills takes practice, this workbook is designed as a comprehensive guide to proven methods for positive change.

This easy-to-read workbook will help people become more aware of their readiness to consider change. Change is hard and most people have mixed feelings or even fears about the unknown. While resistance to change is natural and normal, new awareness can motivate people to contemplate and prepare for the action phase of change. The motivational exercises are designed to help people navigate the change process at a pace that is right for them. For motivational purposes, the exercises are intentionally designed to be short, sweet and easy-to-complete.

Tools and Techniques for the Toolbox

The *CBT Skills Workbook* includes a wealth of step-by-step tips, tools, strategies, practice exercises, activities, handouts and homework assignments. The exercises and worksheets are designed to provide professionals with a practical set of tools that can be used in the sessions, in a group or as homework assignments. The step-by-step easy-to-understand instructions make the exercises easy for clients to understand and complete. Providing a brief rationale for the workbook and the practice exercises will help clients connect with the positive value and reward of completing the short exercises. Completing the exercises will increase motivation and awareness and help clients experience new ways of thinking, feeling, and acting.

The Four Parts

The *CBT Skills Workbook* is divided into four parts or sections. The first section is the ***Motivational Strategies and Skills Section*** which includes exercises and worksheets designed to help clients explore their current level of motivation or readiness to change. The exercises are designed to enhance motivation to change and strengthen commitment to the change process. By exploring the pros and cons of behavioral change and completing the personal values exercises, clients will experience the discrepancy between where they are in life and where they want to be. The nonjudgmental exercises recognize that change is difficult and help clients learn how to take one small step toward change at a time. As explained by Miller & Rollnick, founders of *Motivational Interviewing*, MI prepares and motivates people for change (Miller and Rollnick, 2002).

The second part is the ***Cognitive Therapy Strategies and Skills Section*** which includes a wealth of exercises designed to help people self-discover how their thoughts and beliefs influence their feelings and behaviors. The cognitive therapy worksheets will help clients develop the skills to identify their automatic thoughts, evaluate the accuracy of these thoughts, and develop more realistic and balanced ways of thinking. From goal setting to identifying cognitive distortions, the exercises include the top cognitive therapy tools and techniques designed to help people feel better by changing what they think and do.

The third section is the ***Feeling Better Strategies and Skills Section*** which includes exercises and worksheets designed to help people identify their moods and feelings along with the situations that trigger these moods. Worksheets are specifically designed to aid people in learning how to manage or regulate their emotions right at the time when they are feeling the intensity of emotional pain. The feeling better strategies exercise is a creative worksheet designed to assist people in custom designing their own personal plan for regulating and managing moods and feelings. Feeling better is a key outcome in CBT.

The fourth section is the ***Behavioral Therapy Strategies and Skills Section*** which includes the exercises and worksheets designed to facilitate people in discovering the positive power of learning how to increase positive behaviors. Key exercises and strategies include problem solving, relaxation training, mindfulness practices, exposure strategies, self-esteem training, self-affirmation therapy, assertiveness training, weight loss, and increasing pleasurable activities.

Highlights of the behavioral section include the multiple positive action plans for increasing positive new behaviors like assertiveness, self-esteem, pleasurable activities, and reducing negative behaviors like procrastination, guilt, shame, depression and anxiety. The brief goal-directed action plans include activities that help people brainstorm action steps to help them reach their goals. Key to this book and behavioral therapy is the need for regular practice and rehearsal to shape new behaviors. With encouragement and reward, people can learn more effective self-control strategies to reduce harm and increase positive behavioral choices.

Purpose

The exercises in the *CBT Skills Workbook* are designed to be used as homework between sessions, as structured activities in groups, in treatment programs, and during the counseling sessions. Professionals can combine worksheets into a treatment plan that includes motivational, cognitive, and behavioral exercises and activities or skip around and use exercises and worksheets that match the client's readiness and motivation or present problem. Providing a rationale for the exercises and worksheets, and client readiness are always important factors when introducing these skill-building exercises. It is suggested that clients have their own copy of the workbook as an adjunct to the therapy process.

Who will Benefit from the *CBT Skills Workbook?*

The *CBT Skills Workbook* is especially designed to be used by nurses, counselors, case managers, social workers, marriage and family therapists, graduate students, drug court professionals, criminal justice professionals, addiction counselors, psychiatrists, psychologists, prevention specialists, guidance counselors, their clients, and other consumers interested in treatment, therapy, self-help, personal change, and self-improvement. It can also be used by treatment providers and agencies interested in using cognitive-behavioral approaches with their clients.

It is strongly advised and recommended that the tools and techniques in this workbook be used by people who are in treatment or therapy with a trained and qualified mental health professional.

Directory of Exercises and Worksheets

Part One: Motivational Strategies and Skills 1

Identify Personal Strengths and Supports 3
Identify Stage of Change 4
Decisional Balance Worksheet 5
Costs and Benefits of Changing or Not Changing 6
Ready, Willing and Able 7
Weighing the Risks & Benefits of Change 8
Increasing Confidence to Change 9
Characteristics of Successful Changers 10
Increasing Change Talk 11
Retrain Your Brain: Recipe Cards for Change 12
Weighing the Pros and Cons of

      Change 13
      Intimate Relationships 14
      Parent-Child Relationships 15
      Family Relationships 16
      Worry 17
      Depression 18
      Anxiety 19
      Drinking Alcohol 20
      Smoking 21
      Using Cannabis 22
      Taking Prescription Medications 23
      Procrastination 24
      Expressing Anger 25
Menu of Change Options 26
Consider the Consequences of Action and Inaction 27
Readiness to Accept Things You Can't Change 28
Accepting Things You Can't Change 29
Preparing a Change Plan 30
Describing Your Plans or Intentions to Change 31
Identify Your Important Personal Values 32

Part Two: Cognitive Therapy Strategies and Skills 33

Orientation to Cognitive Therapy 35
Identify Thoughts, Feelings and Behaviors 36
Identify Your Coping Strategies 37
Goal Setting Strategies 38
Designing Action Plans to Reach Goals 39
Setting Goals: Picture Life in Five Years 40
Setting Goals: Visualize Success in Your Life 41

Setting Goals & Monitoring Progress...42

Identify and Label Cognitive Distortions...43

Self-Monitor Automatic Thoughts...44

Four Key CBT Questions...45

The CBT Thought Record..46

Step One: Identify Automatic Thoughts 47

Step Two: Examine the Evidence 48

Step Three: Develop New Balanced Thoughts 49

Develop New Alternative Balanced Thoughts 50

Feel Better by Changing What You Think and Do.......................................51

Retrain the Brain: The Stop & Think Technique 52

Thought-Stopping Techniques 53

Develop the Habit of Positive Thinking...54

Look for the Silver Lining: Turning Adversity to Advantage 55

Feel Better with the ABC Technique 56

Ask Three Questions to Challenge Irrational Beliefs 57

The Power of Positive Self-Talk 58

Reduce Worry: Consider the Odds...59

Schedule Worries 60

Re-Attribution Therapy for Shame and Guilt 61

Exercises and Worksheets on Core Beliefs

    Identify Core Beliefs...62

    Identify Negative Core Beliefs..63

    Modify Negative Core Beliefs...64

    The Pros and Cons of Core Beliefs...65

    Identify Positive Core Beliefs 66

    Strengthen Positive Core Beliefs 67

Part Three: Feeling Better Strategies and Skills

Part Three: Feeling Better Strategies and Skills 69

Identify and Label Your Feelings in the Past 30 Days 71

Identify and Label Your Feelings in the Past Year 72

Identify and Rate Your Feelings Over Your Lifetime..................................73

Self-Monitor: Discover How You Feel..74

Identify Situations that Trigger Moods & Feelings 75

Feeling Better Strategies Handout 76

Feeling Better Strategies Worksheet 77

Positive Action Plan: Improve Your Mood...78

Grounding & Self-Soothing Strategies 79

Coping with Frustration 80

Part Four: Behavior Therapy Strategies and Skills

Part Four: Behavior Therapy Strategies and Skills 81

Problem Identification Worksheet..83

Generating Options to Solve Problems..84

Problem Solving:

    Step One...85

    Step Two...86

Step Three 87

Step Four 88

The Positive Power of Self-Reward 89

Small Step Success Therapy 90

Relaxation Training

Develop Good Breathing Habits 91

Progressive Muscle Relaxation 92

Visualizations and Imagery 93

Reduce Anxiety and Worry: Engage in Absorbing Activities 94

Gradual Exposure to Feared Situations 95

Self-Affirmation Therapy 96

Mindfulness Practices 97

Increase Positive Behaviors with Behavioral Contracts 98

Self-Monitoring Habits You Want to Modify or Change 99

Behavioral Activation: Increase Pleasurable Activities 100

Positive Action Plans

Act More Assertive 101

Increase Self-Esteem 102

Reduce Procrastination 103

Reduce Depression 104

Improve Medication Adherence 105

Reduce Anxiety 106

Reduce High-Risk Drinking 107

Reduce Relationship Problems 108

Reduce Guilt and Shame 109

Anger Management Strategies 110

Increase Social Supports 111

Reduce Feelings of Inferiority 112

Reduce Avoidance 113

Manage Stress 114

Increase Physical Activity 115

Improve Eating Habits 116

Lose Weight 117

Increase Exercise 118

Improve Sleeping Habits 119

Improve Parenting Practices 120

Improve Intimate Relationships 121

Improve Family Relationships 122

Improve Social Skills 123

Improve Positive Coping Skills 124

Cope with Memories of Trauma 125

Cope with Grief and Loss 126

Relapse Prevention

Identify Relapse Warning Signs 127

Recovery Support Plan 128

References 129

Personal Notes and Reflections 135

Part One:

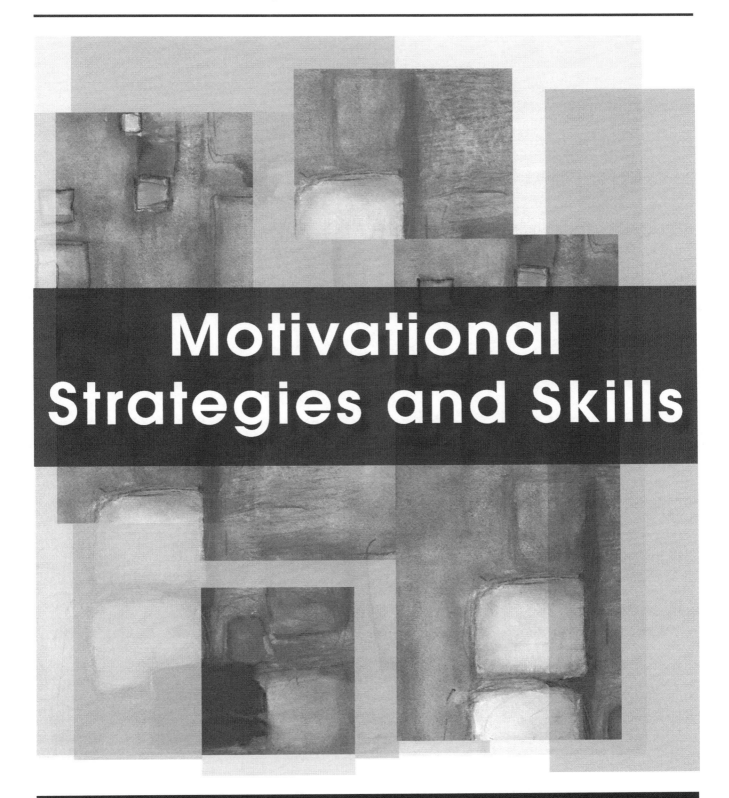

Motivational Strategies and Skills

Exercises and Worksheets

Identify Personal Strengths and Supports

Identifying personal strengths and supports can help people grow and succeed in all areas of life. Identifying personal strengths reminds people that they have personality traits or tools to cope with challenges while identifying support systems can help people remember they are not alone and have other people to turn to for encouragement and support. After creating this list, create a regular way to remind yourself of your strengths and the people in your support system.

List Four Personal Strengths

1. _____

2. _____

3. _____

4. _____

List Four People in Your Support System

1. _____

2. _____

3. _____

4. _____

Identify Stage of Change

Stage of change refers to a person's readiness or motivation to modify or change something in their life. Identifying your state of readiness can greatly enhance your progress in considering change. First answer the question about your motivation and then check the stage that best reflects your current stage of motivation regarding a concern or change you have been thinking about. Remember there is no right or wrong, good or bad thing about your state of readiness.

On a scale of 1-10,
how motivated are you to change?

1 2 3 4	5 6 7	8 9 10
Not Ready	Thinking About It	Ready

Identify Your Stage of Change

	Pre-contemplation:	√	Not yet considering change.
	Contemplation:	√	Considering change.
	Preparation:	√	Planning and committing to change.
	Action:	√	Making the behavior change.
	Maintenance:	√	Maintaining and sustaining change.
	Relapse:	√	I slipped or returned to the behavior.

Decisional Balance Worksheet

People have mixed feelings about change. Old habits are hard to change. Part of us wants to change the other part wants to stay the same. Exploring these mixed feelings or ambivalence is designed to help people tip the scale in the direction of change. Exploring the good and not-so-good things about a self-defeating behavior can create a discrepancy between where you are and where you want to be.

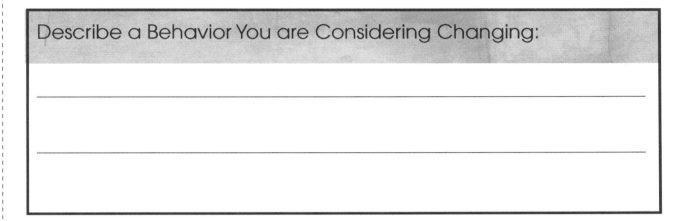

Describe a Behavior You are Considering Changing:

_____

_____

_____

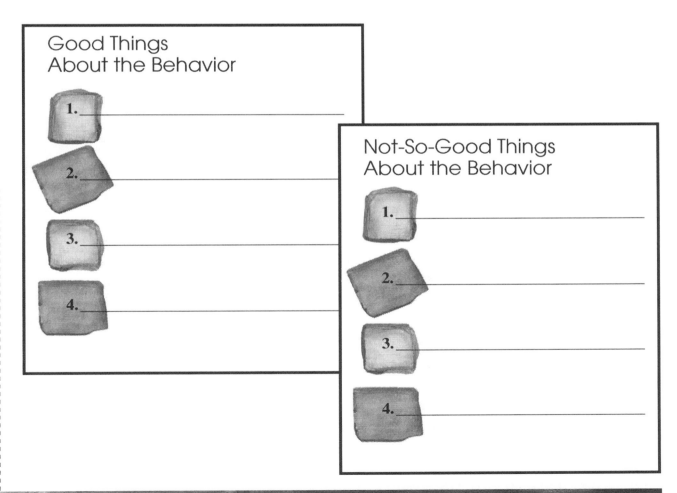

Good Things
About the Behavior

1. _____

2. _____

3. _____

4. _____

Not-So-Good Things
About the Behavior

1. _____

2. _____

3. _____

4. _____

Costs and Benefits of Changing or Not Changing

Describe a behavior you are considering changing and then complete the decisional balance exercise below to help you explore the pros and cons of changing versus not changing. While not changing can help to reduce anxiety, it can also produce unintended consequences like continued pain from not changing.

Describe a Behavior You are Considering Changing:
_____
_____
_____

Deciding to Change

Changing	Not Changing
Costs	Costs
1._____	1._____
2._____	2._____
3._____	3._____
Benefits	Benefits
1._____	1._____
2._____	2._____
3._____	3._____

Ready, Willing and Able

Readiness rulers are designed to help people become more aware of where they are in terms of readiness, willingness and confidence about change. People change when they are ready, willing and confident about making the change.

> ## Describe a Change You are Considering:
>
> _____
>
> _____

On a scale of 1-10, how ready are you to make this change?

On a scale of 1-10, how willing are you to make this change?

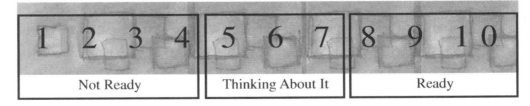

On a scale of 1-10, how confident are you that you can change?

Weighing the Risks & Benefits of Change

Changing is not easy; however, not changing can have unpleasant consequences. Increasing awareness about risks and benefits of changing can motivate people to consider change. A risk/reward analysis can be used with health behaviors like smoking tobacco, drinking alcohol, overeating, not exercising, as well as other habits like destructive expressions of anger, worry, and procrastination.

Describe a Behavior or Habit You Want to Change:

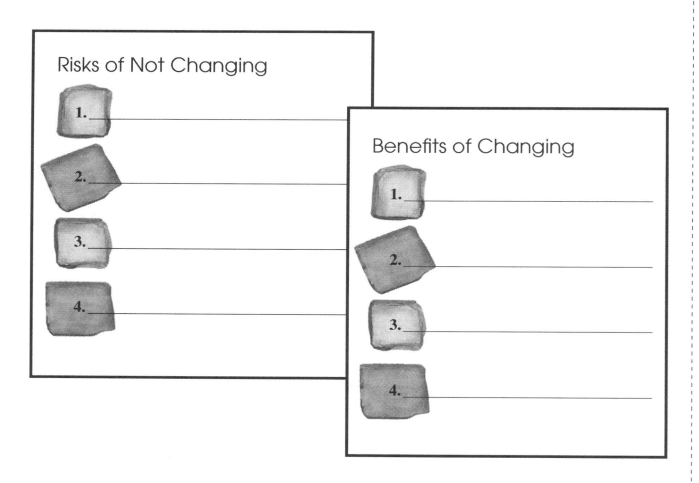

Risks of Not Changing

1.
2.
3.
4.

Benefits of Changing

1.
2.
3.
4.

Increasing Confidence to Change

A strong predicator of successful change is self-efficacy or the belief that people can take the steps to make a desired change. Past history of success and a review of your strengths can increase your self-confidence or self-efficacy. An "I can do it" attitude increases your chances of success.

Describe a Change You are Considering:

1. _____
2. _____
3. _____

Describe Situations in the Past Where You Were Successful at Change

1. _____
2. _____
3. _____

List Your Strengths that Will Help You Change

1. _____
2. _____
3. _____

Characteristics of Successful Changers

People who are successful at making important changes in their lives have characteristics that help increase their confidence about making these changes. Brainstorm and make a list of characteristics of successful changers.

List 10 Characteristics of Successful Changers

1. _____

2. _____

3. _____

4. _____

5. _____

6. _____

7. _____

8. _____

9. _____

10. _____

Increasing Change Talk

Change talk is speech or language that reflects people's desire for or movement toward change. The more people talk about changing the more likely change will happen. The exercises below are designed to help people increase self-motivational statements.

List Any Disadvantages of a Current Problem

1. _____

2. _____

List Any Advantages of Change

1. _____

2. _____

Describe Your Intentions to Change

1. _____

2. _____

Describe Your Optimism About Change

1. _____

2. _____

(Miller and Rollnick, 2002)

Retrain Your Brain: Recipe Cards for Change

One of the most difficult parts of changing old habits is practicing new ones. Bad habits often become hot-wired in the brain making change difficult. One brain-friendly tool to help people learn and frequently practice new skills is using recipe change cards. Just like your grandmother's favorite recipes, you can create your own reminder cards. Written, visual, colorful index cards help to reinforce the change process. After completing your recipe cards, put them on a bulletin board, a mirror, in a recipe box, or on the refrigerator and READ THEM DAILY.

Recipe Card for Losing Weight

Lose Weight
√   Drink more water.
√   Take a walk once per day.
√   Practice mindful eating.
√   Identify trigger foods.
√   Journal feelings before eating.

Recipe Card for Reducing Worry

Reduce Worry
√   List the good things about worry.
√   Self-monitor worries.
√   Schedule worries.
√   List coping strategies.
√   Reframe anxious thoughts.

Weighing the Pros & Cons of Change

One of the most helpful suggestions for changing an unwanted habit or a self-defeating behavior is by looking at the good and not-so-good things about the behavior. People are often motivated to consider change when they perceive a discrepancy between where they are and where they want to be in life.

Exploring the Pros and Cons of Considering Change

Reasons for Staying the Same

Good Things About the Behavior

1._____

2._____

Negative Things About the Behavior

1._____

2._____

Reasons for Making a Change

Good Things About a Change

1._____

2._____

Negative Things About a Change

1._____

2._____

(Miller and Rollnick, 2002)

The Pros & Cons in Intimate Relationships

One of the more helpful suggestions for making improvements in relationships is increasing awareness of the good and not-so-good things in that relationship. People are more motivated to consider change when they perceive a discrepancy between where they are and where they want to be in a relationship.

The Good and Not-So-Good Things in Your Intimate Relationship

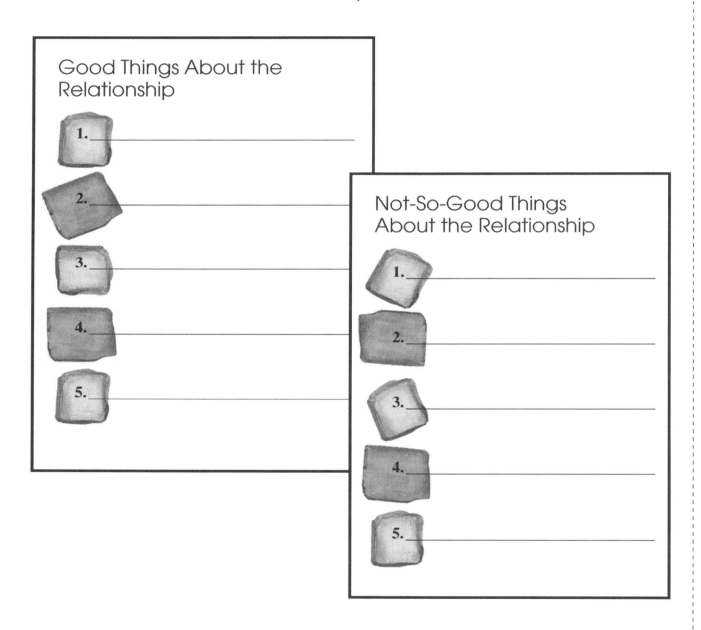

Good Things About the Relationship

1. _____
2. _____
3. _____
4. _____
5. _____

Not-So-Good Things About the Relationship

1. _____
2. _____
3. _____
4. _____
5. _____

The Pros & Cons in Parent-Child Relationships

One of the more helpful suggestions for making improvements in parent-child relationships is increasing awareness of the good and not-so-good things in that relationship. People are more motivated to consider change when they perceive a discrepancy between where they are and where they want to be in a relationship.

The Good and Not-So-Good Things in Your Parent-Child Relationships

Good Things About the Relationship

1. _____

2. _____

3. _____

4. _____

5. _____

Not-So-Good Things About the Relationship

1. _____

2. _____

3. _____

4. _____

5. _____

The Pros & Cons in Family Relationships

One of the more helpful suggestions for making improvements in family relationships is increasing awareness of the good and not-so-good things in that relationship. People are more motivated to consider change when they perceive a discrepancy between where they are and where they want to be in a relationship.

The Good and Not-So-Good Things in Your Family Relationships

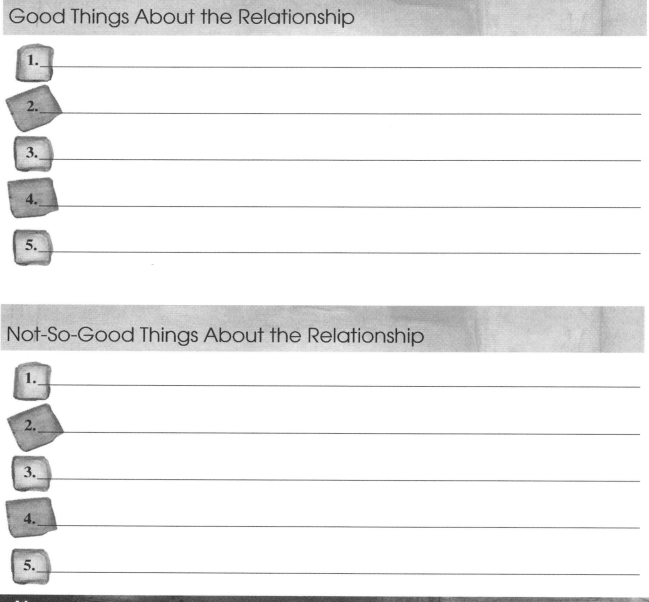

Good Things About the Relationship

1. _____

2. _____

3. _____

4. _____

5. _____

Not-So-Good Things About the Relationship

1. _____

2. _____

3. _____

4. _____

5. _____

The Pros & Cons of Worry

One of the more helpful suggestions for reducing worry is looking at the good and not-so-good things about worry. People are more motivated to consider change when they perceive a discrepancy between where they are and where they want to be including with worry. There are good things about worry.

The Good and Not-So-Good Things About Worry

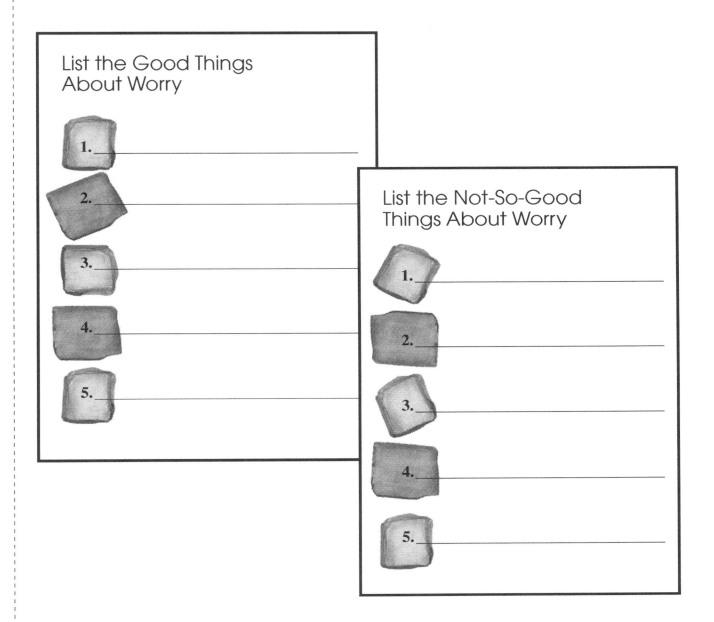

List the Good Things About Worry

1. _____
2. _____
3. _____
4. _____
5. _____

List the Not-So-Good Things About Worry

1. _____
2. _____
3. _____
4. _____
5. _____

The Pros & Cons of Depression

One of the more helpful suggestions for reducing depression is by looking at the "good" and not-so-good things about depression. Good does not mean good in the traditional sense; good means some of the secondary gains or unnoticed aspects of depression that maintain the behavior. People are often motivated to consider reducing or modifying behaviors associated with depression like isolation and inactivity when they perceive a discrepancy between where they are and where they want to be including with the painful feelings of depression.

The Good and Not-So-Good Things About Depression

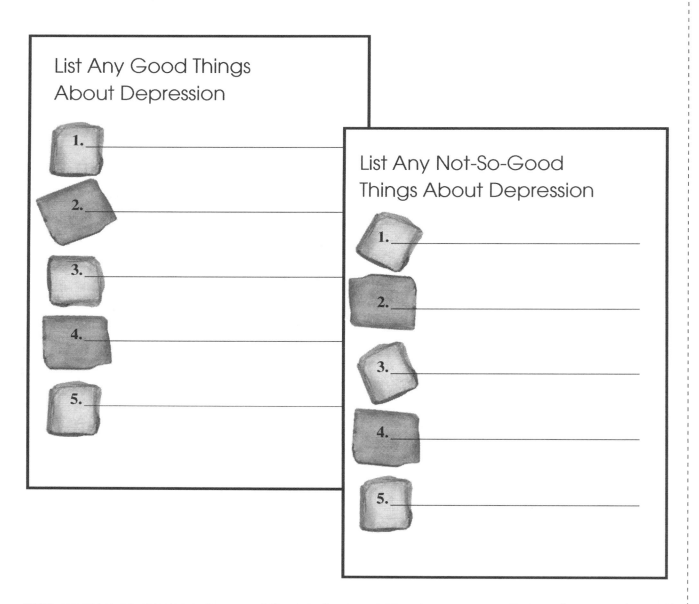

List Any Good Things
About Depression

1.
2.
3.
4.
5.

List Any Not-So-Good
Things About Depression

1.
2.
3.
4.
5.

The Pros & Cons of Anxiety

One of the more helpful suggestions for reducing anxiety is looking at the good and not-so-good things about anxiety. Avoiding fearful situations has both costs and benefits. People are often more motivated to consider change when they perceive a discrepancy between where they are and where they want to be including with anxiety.

The Good and Not-So-Good Things About Anxiety

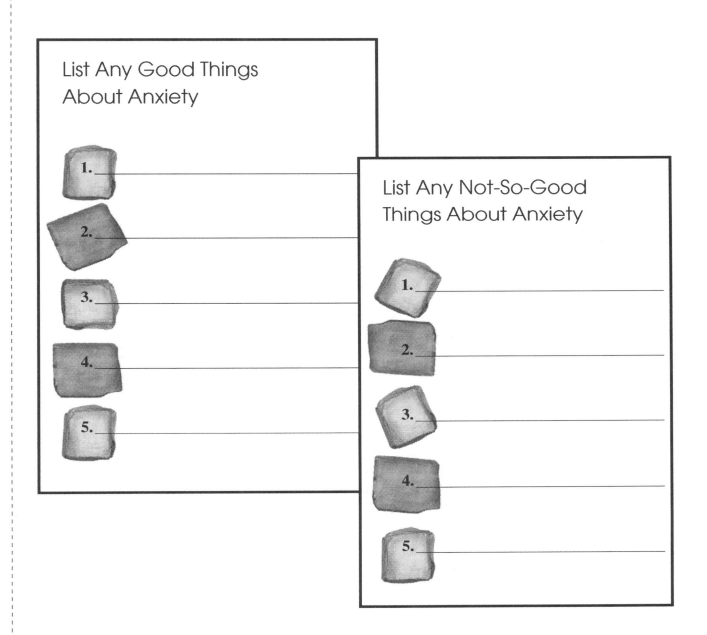

List Any Good Things
About Anxiety

1. _____
2. _____
3. _____
4. _____
5. _____

List Any Not-So-Good
Things About Anxiety

1. _____
2. _____
3. _____
4. _____
5. _____

The Pros & Cons of Drinking Alcohol

One of the more helpful suggestions for making changes in drinking behaviors is looking at the good and not-so-good things about your drinking. People are more motivated to consider change when they perceive a discrepancy between where they are and where they want to be with their drinking habits and patterns.

The Good and Not-So-Good Things About Drinking Alcohol

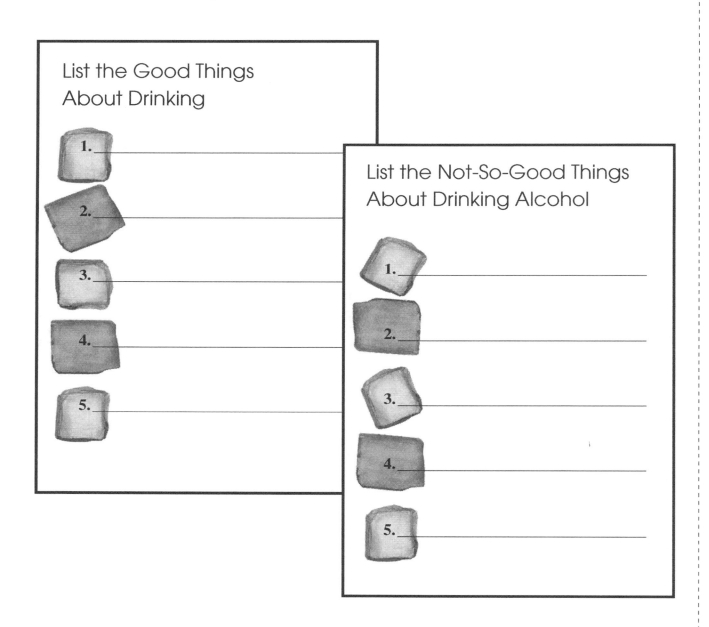

List the Good Things
About Drinking

1. _____
2. _____
3. _____
4. _____
5. _____

List the Not-So-Good Things
About Drinking Alcohol

1. _____
2. _____
3. _____
4. _____
5. _____

The Pros & Cons of Smoking

One of the hardest habits to kick is smoking cigarettes. One of the most helpful suggestions for increasing motivation to quit is looking at the good and not-so-good things about smoking. People are more motivated to consider change when they perceive a discrepancy between where they are and where they want to be with their smoking.

The Good and Not-So-Good Things About Smoking

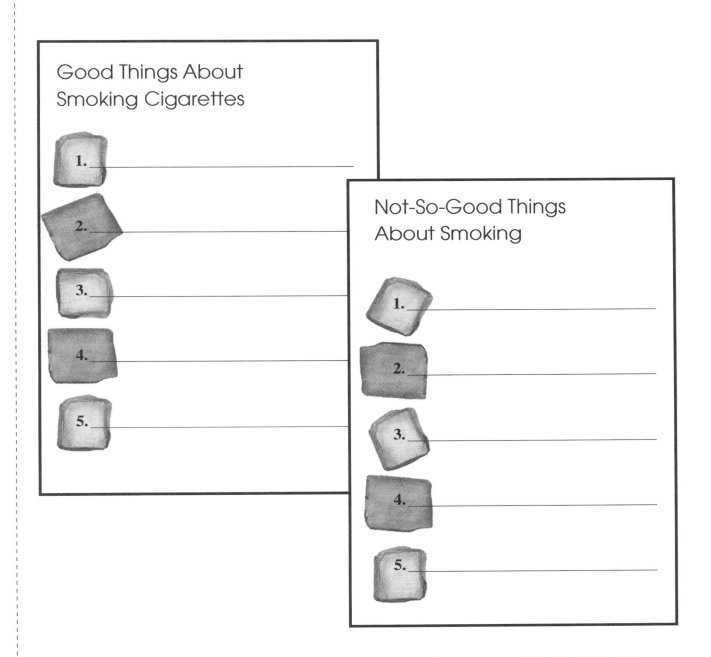

Good Things About
Smoking Cigarettes

1. _____
2. _____
3. _____
4. _____
5. _____

Not-So-Good Things
About Smoking

1. _____
2. _____
3. _____
4. _____
5. _____

The Pros & Cons of Using Cannabis

One of the more helpful nonjudgmental suggestions for making any changes in people's use of marijuana is looking at the good and not-so-good things about smoking cannabis. People are more motivated to consider change when they perceive a discrepancy between where they are and where they want to be including smoking marijuana.

The Good and Not-So-Good Things About Smoking Cannabis

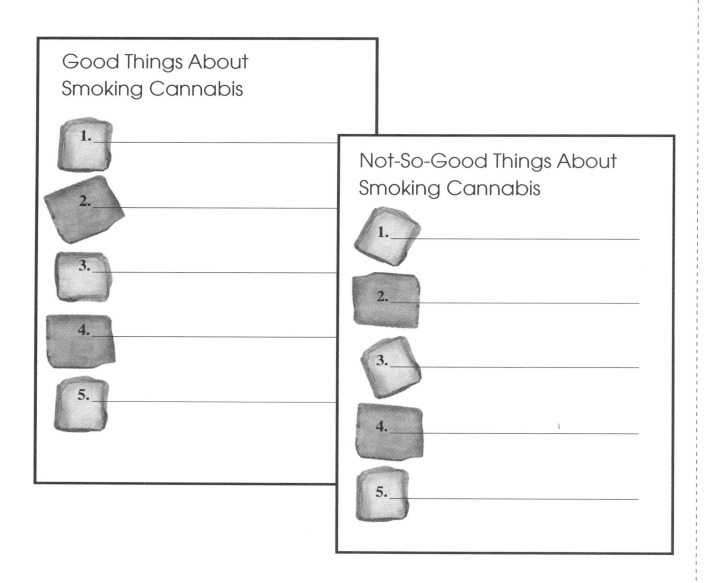

Good Things About Smoking Cannabis

1. _____
2. _____
3. _____
4. _____
5. _____

Not-So-Good Things About Smoking Cannabis

1. _____
2. _____
3. _____
4. _____
5. _____

The Pros & Cons of Taking Prescription Medications

One of the most helpful suggestions for taking prescribed medications for mental health concerns is looking at the good and not-so-good things about taking medications. Sometimes people struggle to start or continue taking medications due to side effects, financial costs, or stigma. People are more motivated to consider taking their medications as prescribed when they become more aware of how they feel taking or not taking these medications.

The Good and Not-So-Good Things About Taking Medications

Good Things About Taking Your Medications

1. _____

2. _____

3. _____

4. _____

5. _____

Not-So-Good Things About Taking Medications

1. _____

2. _____

3. _____

4. _____

5. _____

The Pros & Cons of Procrastination

One of the most helpful suggestions for attacking procrastination is looking at the good and not-so-good things about procrastination. Procrastination can be a self-defeating behavior that is extremely difficult to change leading to unwanted negative consequences. People are more motivated to consider changing their procrastination habits when they perceive a discrepancy between where they are and where they want to be with this behavioral habit.

The Good and Not-So-Good Things About Procrastination

Good Things About Your Procrastination

1. _____

2. _____

3. _____

4. _____

5. _____

Not-So-Good Things About Procrastination

1. _____

2. _____

3. _____

4. _____

5. _____

The Pros & Cons of Expressing Anger

One of the more helpful suggestions for learning how to reduce destructive expressions of anger is by looking at the good and not-so-good things about how anger is expressed. Anger is a healthy emotion except when it is expressed in a destructive, aggressive and/or violent manner. People are more motivated to consider change when they see a difference between the pros and cons with their current expressions of anger.

The Good and Not-So-Good Things About the Way You Express Anger

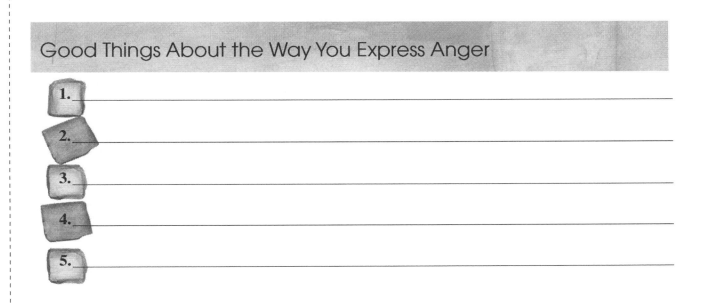

Good Things About the Way You Express Anger

1. _____

2. _____

3. _____

4. _____

5. _____

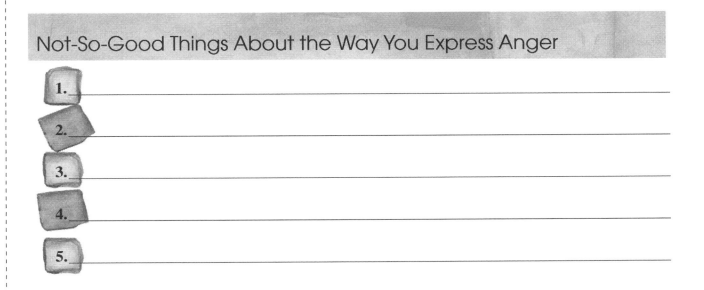

Not-So-Good Things About the Way You Express Anger

1. _____

2. _____

3. _____

4. _____

5. _____

Menu of Change Options

When people consider change to address a difficult problem, listing options provides practical potential options. Brainstorming for options when you are overwhelmed can provide hope. Turning away from the problem and toward your options can dramatically improve your mood and increase your positive choices.

List Your Options

Describe a Problem You are Facing:

_____

_____

_____

What are Your Options?

1. _____

2. _____

3. _____

4. _____

Consider the Consequences of Action and Inaction

Change is not easy, however not changing can have continued negative consequences. This exercise is designed to help you explore the consequences of taking positive action or not taking any action with regard to an area of your life where you a considering change.

List the Consequences of Action or Inaction

Describe a Change You are Considering:

_____

_____

_____

Consequences of Action and Inaction

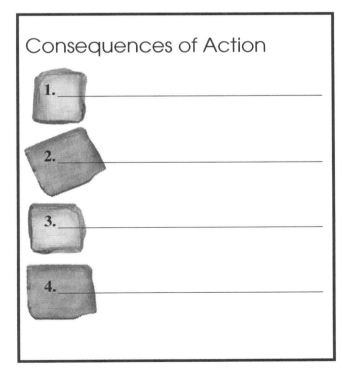

Consequences of Action

1. _____

2. _____

3. _____

4. _____

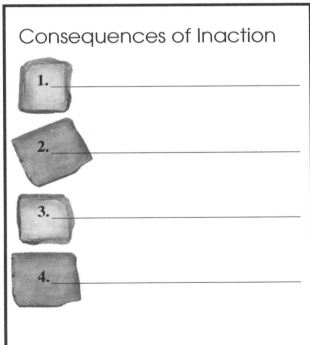

Consequences of Inaction

1. _____

2. _____

3. _____

4. _____

Readiness to Accept Things You Can't Change

Sometimes accepting things we can't change is the best option. Learning to let go means stopping the attempts to change or fix the situation and begin to practice accepting it exactly the way it is. While difficult, letting go can provide increased freedom from the problem. Think about an ongoing long-term situation you have not been able to change and explore below your motivation to consider acceptance as a new alternative way of dealing with the situation.

Describe a situation in your life that you have been trying to change:

_____

_____

On a scale of 1-10, how ready are you
   to let go and accept that you can't change the situation?

On a scale of 1-10, how willing are you
   to let go and accept that you can't change the situation?

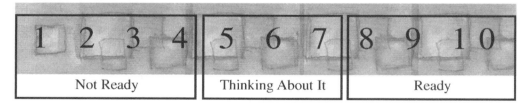

On a scale of 1-10, how confident are you that you
   can let go and accept that you can't change the situation?

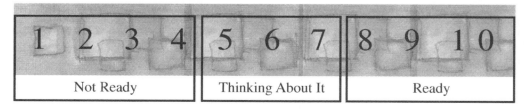

Accepting Things You Can't Change

Sometimes accepting things we can't change is the best option. Learning to let go means stopping attempts to change or fix the situation and begin to practice accepting it exactly the way it is. While difficult, letting go can provide increased freedom from the problem. Make a list of things in your life that you can change or have changed and then a list of things you have tried and most likely can't change. We can learn to accept ourselves and others and to accept our thoughts, feelings and memories instead of trying to change or avoid them.

The Can/Can't Change List

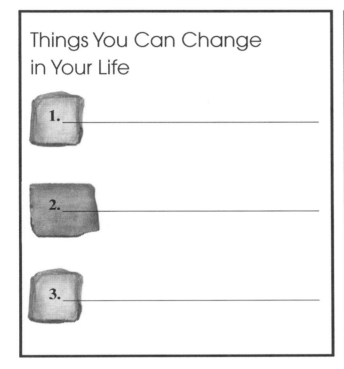

Things You Can Change
in Your Life

1. _____

2. _____

3. _____

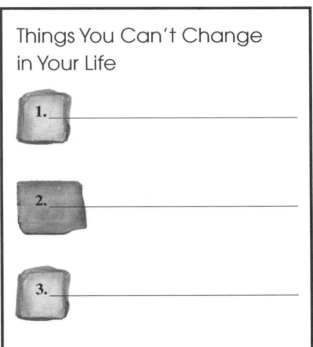

Things You Can't Change
in Your Life

1. _____

2. _____

3. _____

List Ways to Let Go of Things You Can't Change

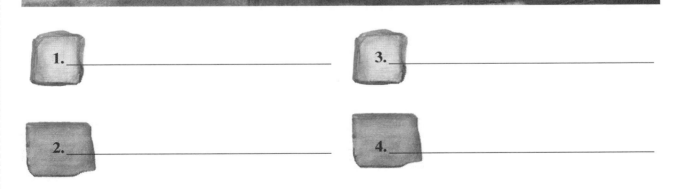

1. _____

2. _____

3. _____

4. _____

Preparing a Change Plan

When considering change, preparing a plan can strengthen your motivation and commitment. Use the outline below to help you develop your own personal plan for change. Refer back to your plan for continued encouragement and support. With your own personal plan you can accomplish whatever you want in life.

Personal Change Plan

The changes I want to make are:

The most important reasons why I want to make these changes are:

My main goals for myself in making these changes are:

I plan to do these things to reach my goals:

The first steps I plan to take in changing are:

Some things that could interfere with my plan are:

Other people could help me change in these ways:

I hope that my plan will have these positive results:

I will know that my plan is working if:

(Miller and Rollnick, 1991)

Describing Your Plans or Intentions to Change

When considering change, describing your plans and intentions can strengthen your motivation and commitment. No one likes to be told how to change, so making up your plan will help reduce any resistance you might have about considering an important change. Refer back to your plan for continued encouragement and support. With your own personal plan you can accomplish whatever you want in life.

Describe a Change You are Considering:

Describe Your Plans and Intentions:

1. _____

2. _____

3. _____

Identify Your Important Personal Values

Identifying personal values can help people set goals and clarify purpose, meaning, and direction in their lives. Values provide direction, especially during difficult or stormy periods of life. Charting a path toward your values can help to create a happier, healthier and more meaningful life. Create a list of your most important values and use this list as a source of inspiration and motivation like a compass or lighthouse during stormy weather. Examples of values include acceptance, autonomy, forgiveness, hope, humor, purpose, tradition, caring or commitment. Make a colorful poster of your personal values code as a visual reminder of what is most important to you in your life.

Identify Your Important Personal Values

1. _____

2. _____

3. _____

4. _____

5. _____

6. _____

7. _____

8. _____

9. _____

10. _____

(Miller, de Braca, & Matthews, 2001)

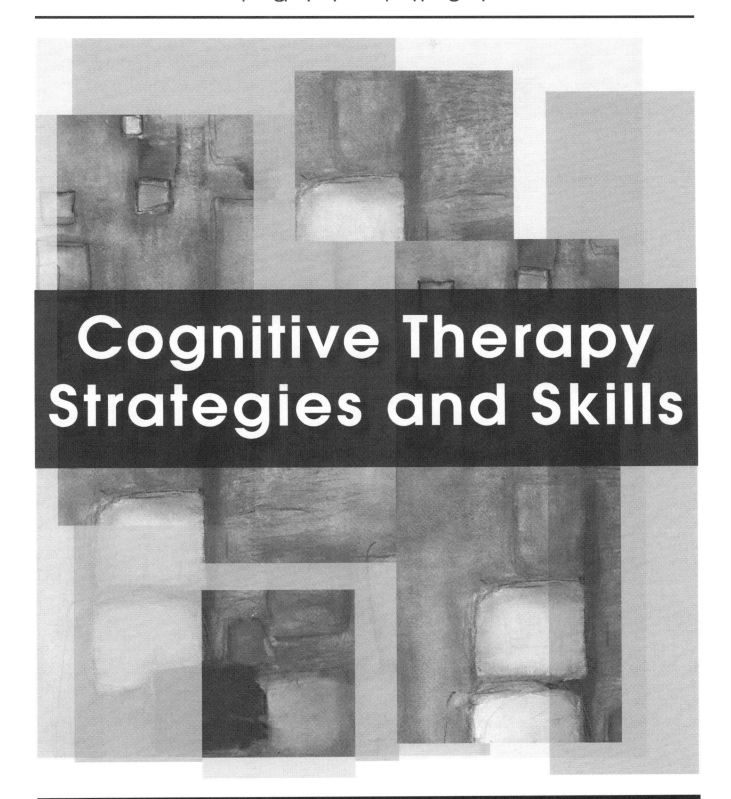

Part Two

Cognitive Therapy Strategies and Skills

Exercises and Worksheets

Orientation to Cognitive Therapy

Cognitive therapy is designed to help people become more aware of the relationship between thoughts, feelings, and behaviors. ***Perceptions of events strongly influence how we feel and act.*** Listed below are three key steps in cognitive therapy including: (1) becoming more aware of automatic thoughts; (2) exploring the evidence that does or does not support an automatic thought; and (3) developing more balanced realistic ways of thinking and believing.

Step 1: **Cognitive Therapy helps people become more aware of the following:**

- Automatic thoughts
- Feelings
- Core beliefs
- Behaviors
- Physical reactions in the body and brain
- The environment

Step 2: **Cognitive Therapy helps people examine the accuracy of their thoughts, assumptions, and beliefs.**

- Thoughts are not facts.
- Examine the evidence.
- Question and challenge irrational beliefs.
- Be a thought detective.
- Don't believe everything you think.
- Look for proof.

Step 3: **Cognitive Therapy helps people develop more positive, realistic, and balanced ways of thinking and believing.**

- Increase your positive self-talk.
- Reduce the ANTS (automatic negative thoughts) in your brain.
- Retrain your brain.
- Replace rational beliefs with more rational ones.
- Cognitive restructuring.
- Changing or modifying thoughts and beliefs.

Identify Thoughts, Feelings, and Behaviors

One way to help people understand their current reactions and patterns is to help them identify the specific thoughts, feelings, behaviors, and physical reactions they have related to everyday, real life situations. This exercise helps people understand how everyday situations trigger thoughts, feelings, and behaviors. Think of a situation in the past month in which you had a strong emotional reaction and describe it below. Next, list the thoughts, feelings, behaviors, and physical reactions in your body you had related to this situation or event.

Describe a Recent Difficult Situation:

_____

_____

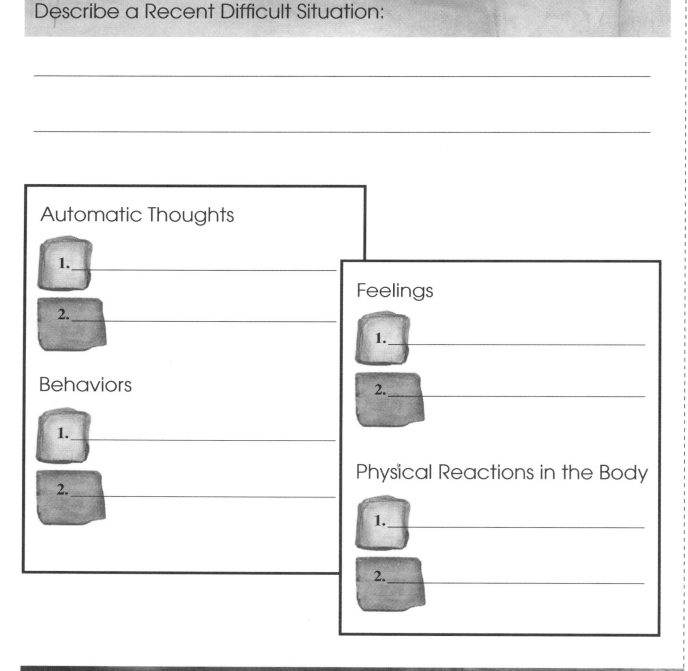

Automatic Thoughts

1. _____

2. _____

Behaviors

1. _____

2. _____

Feelings

1. _____

2. _____

Physical Reactions in the Body

1. _____

2. _____

Identify Your Coping Strategies

People experience both positive and negative challenges in life. Some stressful situations overwhelm our emotions and our ability to cope or deal with them. One helpful suggestion to improve coping ability is to identify the strengths of your current coping style. By listing the good and not-so-good ways of coping with stress and strong emotions, you can increase your awareness of what works and what doesn't work. Remember that the focus is not on right or wrong, but on what works and what is more useful and helpful for you in coping with life's toughest challenges.

Identify Your Current Coping Strategies

List Your Good Coping Strategies

1. _____

2. _____

3. _____

4. _____

List Your Not-So-Good Coping Strategies

1. _____

2. _____

3. _____

4. _____

Goal Setting Strategies

Goal setting techniques are designed to help people develop realistic plans for achieving desired goals in life. Setting goals can provide both a vision and direction to help people make improvements or changes. Goals should be both timely and measurable. Goal setting can also significantly improve motivation as reaching a goal is rewarding. Think of some area of your life where you would like for things to be different or better. Listing action steps will provide a map with specific directions to help ensure that you get where you want to go.

Melt Problems Away By Setting Goals

Goal One:

Positive Action Steps to Reach Your Goal

1. _____

2. _____

3. _____

Goal Two:

Positive Action Steps to Reach Your Goal

1. _____

2. _____

3. _____

Designing Action Plans To Reach Goals

Listing the steps to reach a goal will help to increase your success. Writing down the goal and steps helps to strengthen commitment and motivation. A journey of a thousand miles begins with one step. List your goal and brainstorm steps you will take to reach your goals.

Describe Your Goal:

Positive Action Plan: List 3 Steps to Reach Your Goal

 1. _____

2. _____

3. _____

Setting Goals: Picture Life in Five Years

When setting goals or making improvements, having an image or picture in your mind can help people move in a valued or desired direction. Images or pictures can bring things to life and strengthen motivation and commitment to reach a goal. Draw a picture of what you want your life to look like in five years. After completing your personal drawing, reflect on any differences between your current life and the life you want to have in the future. Drawing is good for the brain.

Draw a Picture of Your Life in Five Years

Setting Goals:
Visualize Success in Your Life

Sit in a comfortable chair and relax. After you feel relaxed, begin to visualize or think about success in your life. Imagine or visualize what success means to you. You may feel a happy emotion or see an image or a picture of your children. With your eyes closed, just try to visualize or imagine success in your mind. After you have completed the exercise, write down what you visualized or describe what you experienced. Compare your visualization with your actual life and notice any differences.

Describe How You Visualize Success:

Setting Goals & Monitoring Progress

Setting goals and monitoring progress can help to reinforce success in therapy. It can also help to identify roadblocks and provide opportunities to clarify more effective ways to reach goals. Goal scaling is designed to measure progress on a scale of 1-10 to monitor progress and provide feedback about the process of taking steps toward goals.

Monitor Your Progress

List Your Goal:

_____

_____

On a scale of 1-10, how much progress have

you made in reaching your goal?

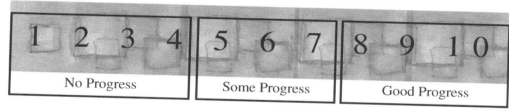

1 2 3 4	5 6 7	8 9 10
No Progress	Some Progress	Good Progress

Reflect on Your Progress:

_____

_____

_____

_____

Identify and Label Cognitive Distortions

Learning about your pattern of thinking can help you catch, modify, or change any distortions or negative thinking errors. Since our thoughts have a strong impact on our feelings and behaviors, there are positive benefits to correcting distorted thinking habits. Listed below are some common cognitive distortions. After reading each description, review your own thinking habits and then answer yes or no if you have ever noticed yourself using the cognitive distortion. Remember, it's not about good or bad or right or wrong it's about becoming more mindful of your thinking patterns.

Cognition Distortion:	Yes/No
Filtering: Focusing only on the negative.	
Polarized thinking; all or nothing thinking.	
Overgeneralization: One negative event means everything is negative.	
Mind-reading: Thinking others are thinking negative things about you.	
Catastrophizing: Expecting disaster.	
Magnifying: Magnifying the size of your problem.	
Should statements: Feeling like you should or must do or not do something.	
Blaming: Attributing blame to yourself.	
Emotional reasoning: Feeling that something is true, therefore it must be true.	
Personalization: Seeing yourself as the cause of a negative event.	
Fortune telling: Making negative predictions.	
Disqualifying the positive: Positive experiences are minimized.	
Labeling: Putting negative labels on self or others.	

From Dr. David Burns, *The Feeling Good Handbook*

Self-Monitor Automatic Thoughts

In cognitive therapy, one of the first steps is to become more aware of automatic thoughts. One suggestion is to record automatic thoughts in a thought diary or journal. At the end of each day, think about any situations in which you had a strong emotional reaction and then list any of the automatic thoughts you remember. Try to list the thoughts without judging the thoughts as right or wrong, good or bad. Describe the situation and list your thoughts.

Day of the Week	Describe the Situation	List Automatic Thoughts
Monday:		
Tuesday:		
Wednesday:		
Thursday:		
Friday:		
Saturday:		
Sunday:		

Four Key CBT Questions

People can use this exercise to understand the connection between life situations, thoughts, feelings, and behaviors. Awareness provides the positive opportunity to modify or change automatic negative thoughts and/or self-defeating behaviors.

Question 1: What Happened?

Describe a situation in the past month in which you had a strong emotional reaction.

_____

_____

Question 2: How Did You Feel?

Describe how you felt directly after the situation happened.

_____

_____

Question 3: What Did You Do?

Describe what you did or how you responded to the situation.

_____

_____

Question 4: What Were You Thinking?

Describe what you were thinking right after this situation.

_____

_____

The CBT Thought Record

This CBT thought record is designed to help people become more aware of the relationship between situations, thoughts, feelings, and behaviors. Think of four situations in the past month in which you had strong emotional reactions. Next, list the situations and your thoughts, feelings, and behaviors related to these situations. Finally, after you complete the thought record go back and look at your thoughts and behaviors in the situations. To change how you feel, change what you do or think. Notice the four key CBT questions in the thought record to help you become more mindful of how situations trigger feelings, thoughts, and behaviors.

The CBT Thought Record

Situations	Feelings	Thoughts	Behaviors
What happened?	How did you feel?	What were you thinking?	What did you do?
1.			
2.			
3.			
4.			

Step One: Identify Automatic Thoughts

Everyday situations in our lives trigger automatic thoughts, feelings, behaviors and physical reactions in the body. Automatic thoughts can be positive or negative and reflect our perceptions of events. It is important to remember that our perceptions or thoughts are not facts. Identifying automatic thoughts can help people change how they feel and act. Think of situations in the past month where you have had strong emotional reactions and then describe the situations, feelings, and automatic thoughts. Awareness is the first step in changing or modifying distorted or self-defeating thoughts and beliefs.

Step One: Identify Automatic Thoughts

Situations	Moods/Feelings	Automatic Thoughts
Describe a recent situation	List feelings	What were you thinking?
• Got stuck in traffic for 2 hours on a hot summer day	• Frustrated • Irritated • Stressed • Annoyed	• Why me? • It's not fair • It's awful • Can't stand it
1.		
2.		
3.		

Step Two: Examine the Evidence

After identifying automatic thoughts in step one, it is helpful to examine the evidence that supports or does not support these automatic thoughts. When people believe thoughts are true, they act and feel like they are true. Depressing or anxious feelings are often triggered by automatic negative and nervous thoughts. By listing the evidence both for and against our own thoughts and beliefs we can learn to get into the habit of more realistic and balanced thinking patterns. More accurate perceptions help us to feel and act better.

Step Two: Examine the Evidence

List an Automatic Thought from Step One:

_____

_____

Thoughts are Not Facts

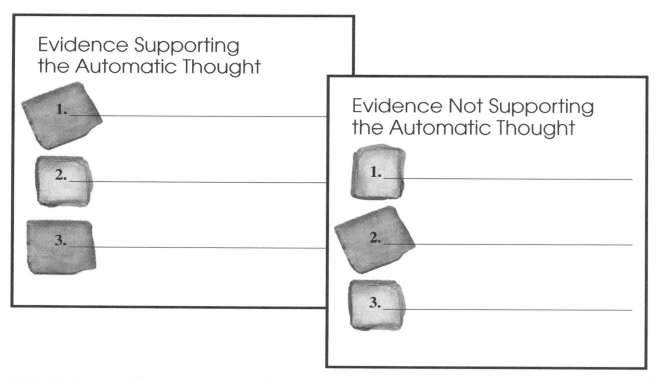

Evidence Supporting
the Automatic Thought

1. _____

2. _____

3. _____

Evidence Not Supporting
the Automatic Thought

1. _____

2. _____

3. _____

Step Three:
Develop New Balanced Thoughts

After examining the evidence of automatic thoughts in step 2, people may discover that the evidence or facts collected do not support the original thought. If the evidence doesn't support the thought, write an alternative or balanced thought. A new balanced thought reflects new evidence and represents a more realistic view of the situation. New alternative balanced thinking leads to significant improvements in how we feel and what we do. After completing and examining the evidence in step two, it's then helpful to generate alternative balanced thoughts. In short, steps 1-3 help people learn how to identify, evaluate, and modify automatic thoughts and beliefs.

List an Automatic Thought from Step One:

_____

_____

Develop Alternative Balanced Thoughts

 1. _____

 2. _____

 3. _____

Develop New Alternative Balanced Thoughts

Thought records are used in cognitive therapy to help people become more aware of the relationship between situations, thoughts, feelings and behaviors. Learning to develop new alternative balanced thoughts is key to changing how you feel and what you do. Describe three situations in the past 6 months in which you had strong emotional reactions and then list your feelings and thoughts. Your first thought may not be completely accurate or helpful so in the final column list what you think are more balanced automatic thoughts and beliefs.

Develop Alternative Balanced Thoughts

Disturbing Situation	Moods/Emotions	Automatic Thoughts	Alternative/Balanced Thoughts
Describe the situation.	List your feelings or moods.	What were you thinking?	Write a more balanced thought.
1.			
2.			
3.			

Feel Better By Changing What You Think and Do

Everyday situations present both positive opportunities and negative situations that significantly impact how we feel and what we do. Our automatic thoughts about events trigger strong emotional reactions and self-defeating behaviors. By modifying or changing what you think or do, you can learn how to feel better. Think of a concern, issue, relationship, situation or problem in your life in which you continue to feel upset or frustrated. Next list 4 positive new thoughts and behaviors that you believe will help you feel better or help solve the problem.

Describe a Situation that Continues to Cause You Emotional Distress:

_____

_____

_____

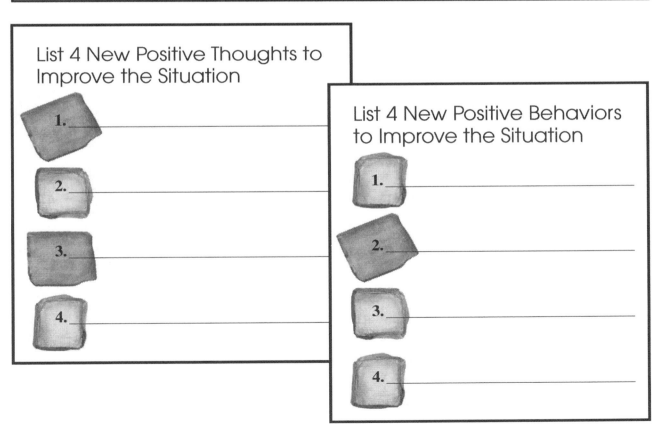

List 4 New Positive Thoughts to Improve the Situation

1. _____

2. _____

3. _____

4. _____

List 4 New Positive Behaviors to Improve the Situation

1. _____

2. _____

3. _____

4. _____

Retrain the Brain:
The Stop & Think Technique

Internal and external events often trigger people to feel and act without thinking. Impulsive actions frequently led to unexpected painful consequences. The first step in the **Stop and Think Technique** is to identify the situations that trigger impulsive behaviors and reactions. Secondly, to help reduce impulsive reactions make a list of positive action steps on an index card. To remind yourself of these new positive thoughts and behaviors repeat the words **Stop and Think**, especially when you are emotionally upset. Repeating these words out loud will help activate your memory of the action steps on your index card. It is also suggested that you display your index cards in highly visible locations as daily friendly reminders for your brain. You may want to practice in front of a mirror to learn the stop and think suggestions faster.

Stop and Think Index Cards

Stop and Think Problem: Destructive Anger

Positive Things I Can do When I am Feeling Angry:

√ Breath and relax

√ Stay calm and cool

√ Walk away

√ Violence is not an option

Stop and Think Problem: Overeating

Positive Things I Can do to Prevent Overeating:

√ Drink water

√ Go for a walk

√ Eat more fruit

√ Call a good friend

√ Avoid trigger foods

Thought-Stopping Techniques

Most people have experienced repeated, unwanted, intrusive or obsessive thoughts running through their minds. Sometimes individuals dwell on people, places and things for hours each day. Unfortunately, automatic thought habits can cause strong emotional reactions, self-defeating behaviors and physical reactions in the body. The thought-stopping techniques listed below are helpful suggestions to help people learn how to distract themselves or reduce or stop automatic unwanted thoughts. After reading the list, make a list on an index card of your favorite thought- stopping techniques.

Close your eyes and shout STOP!

Slap the desk and say the word stop.

Say: "Delete negative thought and replace it."

Visualize a red stop sign.

Think of more pleasant thoughts.

List unwanted thoughts on paper.

Switch to positive thoughts.

Sing your favorite song.

Snap a rubber band worn around the wrist.

Stop and take ten deep slow breaths.

Schedule times of the day to worry.

List Your Favorite Thought-Stopping Techniques

Develop the Habit of Positive Thinking

The habit of realistic positive thinking takes practice. The powerful benefits of positive thinking include: improved mood, increased happiness, more success, increased serenity, peace, more wealth and better health. Suggestions for more positive thinking include: increasing your positive self-talk, expecting positive outcomes, repeating positive affirmations, and practicing positive visualizations. Another proven method of increasing positive thinking is listing positive thoughts and then reading them every day out loud with feeling for support. Create and design your list to help you increase your personal power with more affirming positive self-talk. Make a colorful poster or flyer and post in your favorite place or stand in front of a mirror and say your positive thoughts 5 times out loud. Positive thoughts are good for your brain.

List Ten Important Positive Thoughts to Change & Improve Your Life

1. _____

2. _____

3. _____

4. _____

5. _____

6. _____

7. _____

8. _____

9. _____

10. _____

Look for the Silver Lining: Turning Adversity to Advantage

It is not easy to see any advantages or good things when bad things happen. Unfortunately, the brain stores bad memories from the past and new situations continue to trigger them. However, sometimes when we look back on unpleasant situations we can uncover some good things or the silver lining that came out of the bad situation. List 2 unpleasant events or memories from your past. Next, try to think of any good things that happened after the unpleasant event. Sometimes people get a better job after getting fired. Looking for the silver lining will help to reduce the distress of past painful memories and help you to feel better.

List an Unpleasant Event/Memory from Your Past

Describe Your Silver Lining:

List an Unpleasant Event/Memory from Your Past

Describe Your Silver Lining:

Feel Better with the ABC Technique

The ABC worksheet helps people identify what they say to themselves especially during disturbing events. Everyday situations can trigger unhelpful or irrational ways of thinking which can result in excessive emotional reactions and self-defeating behaviors. Disputing, questioning, and replacing irrational beliefs with rational beliefs helps people feel and act better. Think of a situation in the past month in which you had a strong emotional reaction. List (A) the activating event, (B) your beliefs or thoughts about the event or situation, and (C) the consequences including your feelings and actions. Finally, after questioning and challenging any irrational beliefs, list some more helpful or rational beliefs.

A = Activating Event	B = Irrational Beliefs	C = Consequences
What Happened?	What Did You Say to Yourself?	What Did You Do and How Did You Feel?

List Rational Beliefs:

_____

_____

Ask Three Questions to Challenge Irrational Beliefs

The ability to be more flexible, open-minded, tolerating and accepting is key to rational thinking. Conversely, irrational beliefs can cause excessive emotional reactions and self-defeating behaviors. Learning to question and challenge irrational beliefs and replace those with more rational coping statements can help people to feel and act better. Pick some strongly held thoughts or beliefs and then answer the three rational questions to help you decide if the thoughts or beliefs are helpful or not so helpful.

List Rational Beliefs:

_____

_____

_____

Ask Three Rational Questions

1. Is My Thinking Based on Facts?

_____

_____

2. Does My Thinking Help Me Achieve My Goals?

_____

_____

3. Does My Thinking Help Me Feel the Way I Want to Feel?

_____

_____

The Client's Guide to Cognitive-Behavioral Therapy by Aldo R. Pucci, MA, DCBT

The Power of Positive Self-Talk

What you think or say to yourself about everyday situations in your life will strongly influence how you feel and what you do. Negative self-talk can cause unpleasant emotions and self-defeating behaviors. Replacing automatic negative thoughts with positive self-talk can help you feel and act better. Because thoughts are not facts, it is important to get in the habit of always testing, challenging, disputing, and changing your automatic negative self-talk. In the table below, list any negative thoughts or beliefs you have or had in the past and then replace with some new positive self-talk

"Watch Your Self-Talk"

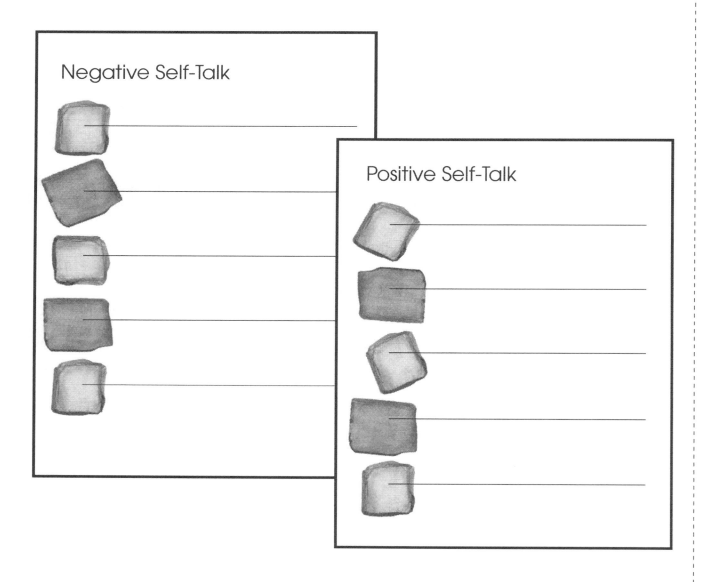

Negative Self-Talk

Positive Self-Talk

Reduce Worry: Consider the Odds

When people are fearful and anxious their brain usually overestimates danger and underestimates its ability to cope with stressful situations. People act and feel as if their worst fears will come true. Reviewing the likelihood or probability on a scale of 1-10 is an effective way to reduce anxiety and worry. Doing the math or considering the odds is good for the anxious brain. After listing a fear or worry, check the number that best reflects your estimation of the likelihood that your fear or worry will happen. Considering the odds is designed to help you learn how to manage fear and worry, without letting it overwhelm you. Remember that some fear and worry is good in helping prepare and protect us from real threats.

Consider the Odds

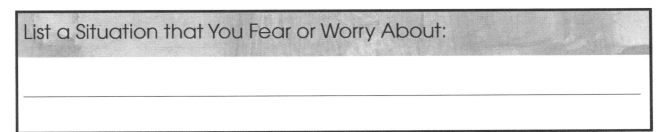

List a Situation that You Fear or Worry About:

On a scale of 1-10, how likely is it the
event you fear or worry about will happen?

1 2 3 4 5 6 7 8 9 10

List a Situation that You Fear or Worry About:

On a scale of 1-10, how likely is it the
event you fear or worry about will happen?

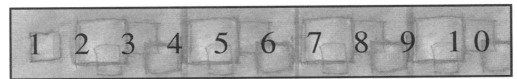

1 2 3 4 5 6 7 8 9 10

Schedule Worries

Worry can help prepare us to take care of health, children, families and responsibilities. However when we worry so much that it makes us sick, it is helpful to learn skills to reduce this excessive chronic type of worry. A helpful technique for people who worry all the time is to schedule 10 to 15 minutes per day to worry. Find a room in the house to sit down and schedule a specific time to devote to important personal worries. Try to notice what you do when you worry and what you do when you leave the room to begin to learn how not to worry. To worry less try different distraction techniques like thought-stopping or engaging in absorbing activities that require concentration.

Schedule a Time and Place to Worry

List Things You Worry About

1. _____

2. _____

3. _____

4. _____

5. _____

Re-Attribution Therapy for Shame and Guilt

People will sometimes only blame themselves or only blame others for their problems. People sometimes think, "it's all his or her fault or it's entirely my fault." Visualizing a pie chart, can help people learn how to distribute responsibility more accurately. List a situation where you blame yourself and feel a deep sense of shame and/or guilt. Next brainstorm and think of other potential factors that are responsible for or have contributed to the situation. Distributing responsibility more accurately is designed to help you reduce your shame or guilt.

Describe a Situation Where You Blamed Yourself:

_____

_____

List Potential Factors that Contributed to the Situation

Identify Core Beliefs

Core beliefs have a strong impact on the quality of our lives including our physical and mental health. These helpful and not-so-helpful core beliefs represent our view of ourselves, others, the world and the future. Learned in childhood and over the lifespan, core beliefs are often rigid, absolute and difficult to change. Identifying negative, self-defeating beliefs can help uncover the root influences on current thoughts, feelings, and behaviors. In the exercise below, describe your current beliefs about yourself, others, and the world. Imagine that your core beliefs act like a filter or a pair of rose colored glasses that enhance or distort your view of yourself, others, and the world.

I am...?

_____

_____

_____

Others are...?

_____

_____

_____

The World is...?

_____

_____

_____

Identify Negative Core Beliefs Worksheet

Dr. Aaron Beck, father of Dr. Judith Beck and founder of cognitive therapy, found that people have specific negative core beliefs about themselves that influence feelings and behaviors. Rate the beliefs below according to what you have believed about yourself since your childhood, using the following 5-point rating scale.

1 = Strongly Agree (SA) 2 = Agree (A) 3 = Neutral (N) 4 = Disagree (D) 5 = Strongly Disagree (SD)

Individual Core Beliefs	1 = SA	2 = A	3 = N	4 = D	5 = SD
I am unlovable.	1	2	3	4	5
I am unattractive.	1	2	3	4	5
I am undesirable.	1	2	3	4	5
I am rejected.	1	2	3	4	5
I am unwanted.	1	2	3	4	5
I am uncared for.	1	2	3	4	5
I am helpless.	1	2	3	4	5
I am inadequate.	1	2	3	4	5
I am powerless.	1	2	3	4	5
I am trapped.	1	2	3	4	5
I am inferior.	1	2	3	4	5
I am incompetent.	1	2	3	4	5
I am weak.	1	2	3	4	5
I am vulnerable.	1	2	3	4	5

Modify Negative Core Beliefs

People often act and feel as if their negative beliefs are 100% true. Negative core beliefs have a strong influence on our everyday lives and relationships. To modify or change them, it is helpful to look for evidence that refutes or disproves them. To weaken a negative core belief, we look very hard every day for evidence or facts that suggest it is not true. To modify a rigid negative core belief, we need to forcefully and actively weaken it with strong compelling counter- evidence and facts.

List the Negative Core Belief:

_____

List Evidence and Facts Not Supporting Your Negative Core Belief

1. _____

2. _____

3. _____

4. _____

5. _____

From: *Mind Over Mood*, Dennis Greenberger & Christine A. Padesky

The Pros and Cons of Core Beliefs

Core beliefs are deeply ingrained in personality and difficult to modify or change. Negative core beliefs can affect thoughts, moods, and behaviors. While people may be unaware of their negative core beliefs, people are aware of the intense emotional pain and self-destructive behaviors. One way to modify these beliefs is to list both the good and the not-so-good things about these beliefs. Try to detach from your feelings about the negative core belief and objectively try to list any good and not-so-good things about the negative core belief.

List a Negative Core Belief:

_____

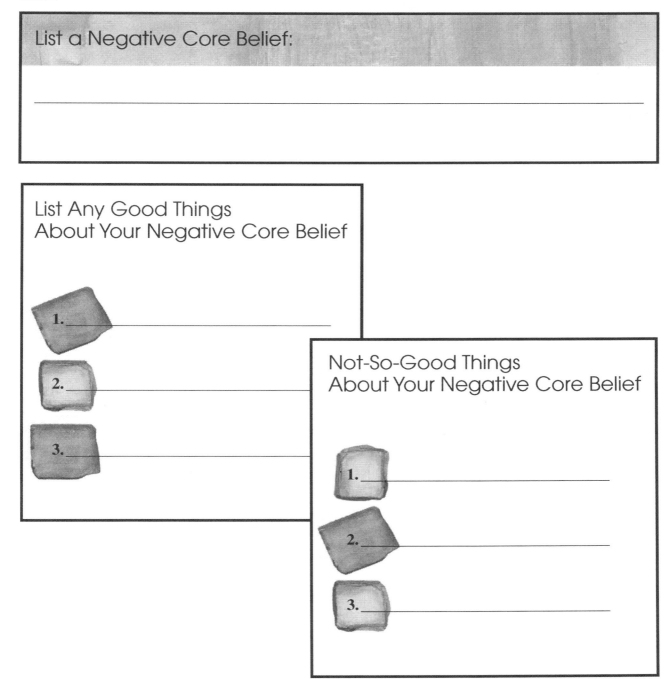

List Any Good Things
About Your Negative Core Belief

1. _____

2. _____

3. _____

Not-So-Good Things
About Your Negative Core Belief

1. _____

2. _____

3. _____

Identify Positive Core Beliefs

According to what you have believed about yourself since your childhood, rate the beliefs below using to the following 5-point rating scale. It is helpful to strengthen positive core beliefs with practice.

1 = Strongly Agree (SA) 2 = Agree (A) 3 = Neutral (N) 4 = Disagree (D) 5 = Strongly Disagree (SD)

Individual Core Beliefs	1 = SA	2 = A	3 = N	4 = D	5 = SD
I deserve love.	1	2	3	4	5
I am a good person.	1	2	3	4	5
I can trust others.	1	2	3	4	5
I am worthwhile.	1	2	3	4	5
I am healthy.	1	2	3	4	5
I am lovable.	1	2	3	4	5
I am deserving.	1	2	3	4	5
I can be trusted.	1	2	3	4	5
I can succeed.	1	2	3	4	5
I am in control.	1	2	3	4	5
I can be myself.	1	2	3	4	5
I am strong.	1	2	3	4	5
I can take care of myself.	1	2	3	4	5
I am smart.	1	2	3	4	5
I am safe.	1	2	3	4	5

Strengthen Positive Core Beliefs

What we say to ourselves has an enormous impact on how we feel and what we do. It is helpful to replace negative core beliefs with more positive beliefs. To strengthen a positive new core belief, every day look hard for evidence or facts that suggest the new beliefs are, in fact, true. To increase your believability in a new positive core belief, actively look for compelling and persuasive facts and evidence that support the new belief. Chipping away at negative core beliefs and believing in positive new core beliefs takes repeated practice and time. It can be helpful to visualize your positive and negative beliefs as images outside of yourself.

List a Positive Core Belief:

_____

List Evidence and Facts that Support a Positive New Core Belief

1. _____

2. _____

3. _____

4. _____

5. _____

From: *Mind Over Mood*, Dennis Greenberger & Christine A. Padesky

Part Three

Feeling Better Strategies and Skills

Exercises and Worksheets

Identify and Label Your Feelings in the Past 30 Days

To learn how to modify, change, or accept how you feel, it is helpful first to identify and label your feelings and moods over the past 30 days. Listed below are words that are associated with the four basic emotions: sad, mad, glad, or scared. Circle, highlight, or check the words below that best describe your moods or feelings in the past 30 days.

Depressed	Anxious	Angry	Guilty	Ashamed
Sad	Embarrassed	Excited	Frightened	Irritated
Insecure	Proud	Mad	Panicky	Frustrated
Nervous	Disgusted	Hurt	Cheerful	Disappointed
Enraged	Scared	Happy	Loving	Humiliated
Helpless	Hopeless	Agitated	Misunderstood	Trapped
Victimized	Worried	Outraged	Grateful	Peaceful
Safe	Worthwhile	Joy	Fearful	Afraid

From: *I Can't Get Over It A Handbook for Trauma Survivors*: Aphrodite Matsakis and Mind Over Mood: Dennis Greenberger and Christine A. Padesky

Identify and Label Your Feelings in the Past Year

To learn how to modify, change, or accept how you feel, it is helpful first to identify and label your feelings and moods in the past year. Listed below are words that are associated with the four basic emotions: sad, mad, glad, or scared. Circle, highlight, or check the words below that best describe your mood or feelings in the past year.

Depressed	Anxious	Angry	Guilty	Ashamed
Sad	Embarrassed	Excited	Frightened	Irritated
Insecure	Proud	Mad	Panicky	Frustrated
Nervous	Disgusted	Hurt	Cheerful	Disappointed
Enraged	Scared	Happy	Loving	Humiliated
Helpless	Hopeless	Agitated	Misunderstood	Trapped
Victimized	Worried	Outraged	Grateful	Peaceful
Safe	Worthwhile	Joy	Fearful	Afraid

From: *I Can't Get Over It A Handbook for Trauma Survivors*: Aphrodite Matsakis and Mind Over Mood: Dennis Greenberger and Christine A. Padesky

Identify and Rate Your Feelings Over Your Lifetime

To learn how to modify, change, or accept how you feel, it is helpful first to identify, label and rate your feelings and moods over your lifetime. Reflect upon your moods and feelings over your lifetime and list five feeling words that best describe these feelings and emotions. Next, rate these feelings and moods on a scale from 1-10, with 1 being the weakest and 10 being the strongest. Use the *Identify and Label Your Feelings Worksheets* to help you select five words that best describe your emotions, feelings, or moods over your lifetime.

Identify and Rate Your Five Lifetime Moods on a Scale of 1-10	
1.	
2.	
3.	
4.	
5.	

Self-Monitoring: Discover How You Feel

Sad, mad, glad, and scared are considered to be the 4 basic emotions. Self-monitoring your feelings for one week can help you identify situations that trigger and maintain your moods. For each day of the week, describe a positive or negative situation in which you remember having a strong emotional reaction. Then check which emotions you felt each time; you can check one, two, or all four emotions.

Day of the Week	Describe the Negative or Positive Situation	Angry	Fearful	Sad	Happy
Monday:					
Tuesday:					
Wednesday:					
Thursday:					
Friday:					
Saturday:					
Sunday:					

Identify Situations that Trigger Moods and Feelings

Positive and negative moods and feelings are connected to everyday situations and our perceptions of these situations. Disturbing or upsetting situations can trigger intense emotional reactions in our bodies and in our behavioral reactions. Sometimes the tidal waves of our emotions can sink us and leave us feeling stuck and overwhelmed. Think about 3 situations in the past month in which you had strong emotional reactions. Next describe the situations and then your feelings and moods. It's also good to record any positive events, moods and feelings.

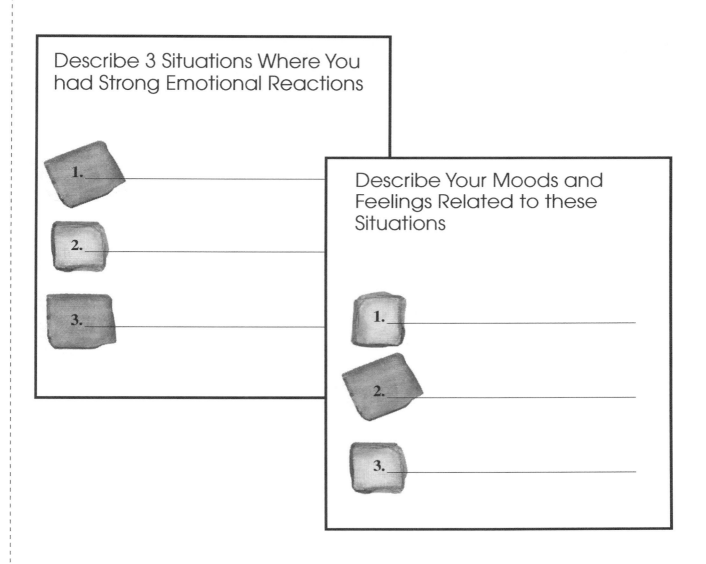

Describe 3 Situations Where You had Strong Emotional Reactions

1.

2.

3.

Describe Your Moods and Feelings Related to these Situations

1.

2.

3.

Feeling Better Strategies Handout

When people are emotionally upset they typically resort to relief-seeking self-defeating strategies. With practice, people can retrain the brain to respond differently to emotional pain. Review the list below and select strategies that are right for you. Writing strategies on large colorful index cards and reviewing them daily will increase your confidence. Visualize the words on the index cards to remind yourself of your feeling better strategies. Doing something when you are overwhelmed with negative emotions will help you turn down the volume on intense moods and feelings.

Make a list of pleasurable things to do.	Develop good sleep routines.
Engage in regular physical exercise.	Take steps to increase physical activity.
Participate in self-growth and development.	Be mindful or aware of your feelings.
Improve relationships.	Solve problems.
Express feelings in a journal.	Manage stress.
Call a friend.	Practice positive self-talk.
Practice deep breathing and relaxation.	Accept your feelings.
Engage in a fun activity.	Reduce automatic negative thoughts.

Feeling Better Strategies Worksheet

Listing ways to feel better is designed to give people a roadmap or direction at times when they are feeling emotionally upset. Strong emotional reactions frequently activate self-defeating behaviors. To increase positive feelings and behaviors, it is helpful to learn ways to feel better. Writing an activity on a large colorful index card will reinforce the ability to learn these feeling better strategies when people need them the most. Visualize the words on the index cards to remind yourself of positive self-talk or action steps to take during times when the emotional part of the brain takes over. To feel better, do something different right when you are feeling bad.

List Things that Make You Feel Good

1. _____

2. _____

3. _____

4. _____

5. _____

Positive Action Plan: Improve Your Mood

Developing a positive action plan can help you change habits and feel better. Listing positive steps will help to increase your confidence so that you can change, accept, improve and feel better. List 4 ways you can take to improve your mood.

Goal: Improve Your Mood

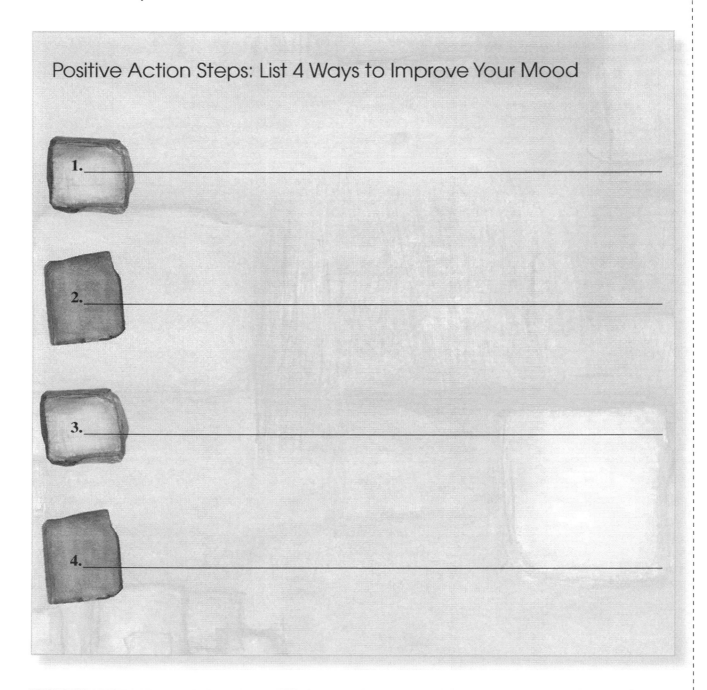

Positive Action Steps: List 4 Ways to Improve Your Mood

1._____

2._____

3._____

4._____

Grounding & Self-Soothing Strategies

Grounding exercises and practices are designed to help people cope with the tidal waves of intense emotional pain. Sometimes situations or memories trigger strong emotional reactions that lead to self-defeating, impulsive or harmful behaviors. Grounding helps people turn down the emotional volume inside the brain by focusing more on soothing activities that help people feel better by focusing on activities outside of the mind. Listed below are some examples of strategies for coping with emotional pain. After reviewing the list, make your own list. A helpful suggestion is to put your self-soothing strategies on colorful index cards and put them in place where you can visually see and read them on a regular basis.

Review Popular Self-Soothing Strategies and Activities

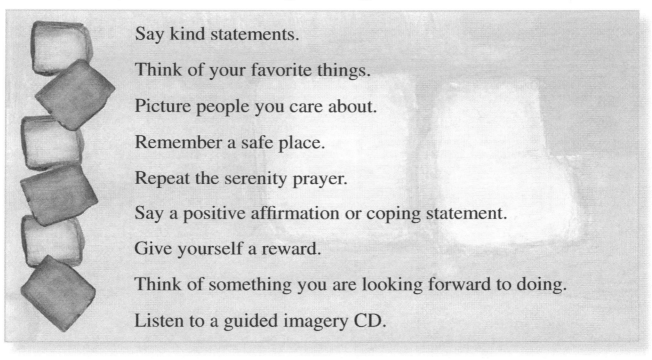

Say kind statements.

Think of your favorite things.

Picture people you care about.

Remember a safe place.

Repeat the serenity prayer.

Say a positive affirmation or coping statement.

Give yourself a reward.

Think of something you are looking forward to doing.

Listen to a guided imagery CD.

List Your Own Grounding or Self-Soothing Strategies

Coping with Frustration

Most people are confronted with frustration or distress in everyday life. Dealing with situations and people that block us can trigger strong emotional reactions like anger and disappointment. Strong emotional pain in the brain can overwhelm people's capacity to successfully cope with intense feelings of frustration. When people are feeling frustrated, they turn to quick fix or relief strategies that often don't work and make matters worse. By making a plan, people can learn to switch gears in the brain and turn toward more rational coping with frustration strategies. It's helpful to make a list when we are calm before the storm.

Create a Coping with Frustration Plan

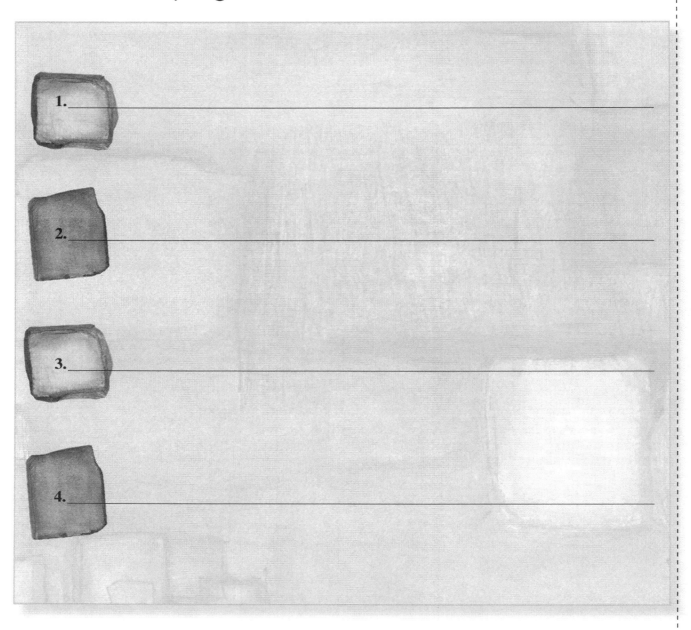

1. _____

2. _____

3. _____

4. _____

Behavior Therapy Strategies and Skills

Exercises and Worksheets

Problem Identification Worksheet

The exercise below is designed to help you become more aware of how you are functioning in key areas or domains of your life. Use the scoring system of 0-4, rate the degree to which you are experiencing concerns or problems in any of the problem domains. You may be doing well in some areas and not so good in other areas.

0 = Not at all   1 = Slightly   2 = Moderately   3 = Considerably   4 = Extremely

Problem Area/Domain	0	1	2	3	4
Medical/health					
Alcohol/drug					
Legal					
Money/financial					
Employment/work					
Living situation					
Partner/spouse relationship					
Parenting/relationship with your children					
Family of origin relationships					
Work relationships					
Leisure/recreation					
Psychological/psychiatric					
Environmental/community					

Generating Options to Solve Problems

Brainstorming potential options is an effective way of looking at a problem from a different perspective. When we are overwhelmed by some of life's toughest challenges, it's easy to lose hope. In brainstorming, the secret is not to evaluate or dismiss an option, but use your creativity to generate multiple ways of solving a problem. Generating options is designed to increase hope and improve problem-solving skills.

Describe a Problem

List Your Options

1. _____

2. _____

3. _____

4. _____

5. _____

Problem-Solving: Step One

Step One: Define the Problem

The first step in problem-solving involves learning how to define a problem in an objective and complete manner. Think about a problem or concern from the past or in the present that is upsetting or bothering you. Pick a problem where you have mixed feelings or feel stuck. To define the problem, write down a description of your perception of the problem.

Briefly Describe a Concern or Problem

_____

_____

_____

_____

_____

Problem Solving: Step Two

Step Two: Brainstorm for Options

After defining the problem, brainstorm potential options. In brainstorming, the secret is not to evaluate or dismiss an option, but use your creativity to generate multiple ways of solving a problem.

List 3 Options to Help You Solve Your Problem

Option 1:

Option 2:

Option 3:

Problem Solving: Step Three

Step Three: Evaluate Your Options

In the third step, list the advantages and disadvantages to help you weigh the pros and cons of each option. As you evaluate your options, you will become more mindful of the solution that is right for you.

Option 1:

Pros:

1._____

2._____

Cons:

1._____

2._____

Option 2:

Pros:

1._____

2._____

Cons:

1._____

2._____

Option 3:

Pros:

1._____

2._____

Cons:

1._____

2._____

Problem Solving: Step Four

Step Four: Put Your Plan into Action

Review the pros and cons of each option and select the best solution for your problem. After selecting an option, it is important to turn your option into positive action. Rate how confident you feel that your option will work to help you solve your problem, issue or concern.

Step 1:

List the option you selected to solve your problem:

_____

_____

Step 2:

Describe action steps you can take to put your plan into action:

_____

_____

Step 3:

On a scale of 1-10, how confident do you feel that your plan will work?

1 2 3 4	5 6 7	8 9 10
Not confident	Somewhat confident	Confident

The Positive Power of Self-Reward

Changing self-defeating behaviors or bad habits is difficult. There are both good and not-so-good things about habits and behaviors. People continue to use drugs because they provide a perceived benefit that outweighs any perceived negative consequences. One helpful way to shape or modify a behavior or learn a new habit is to provide meaningful, positive self-rewards for the new behavior. List below a behavior you want to modify or change, or a new behavior you want to learn. Next make a list of enjoyable rewards including positive material items, positive activities, or positive self-statements. After engaging in the behavior, use one of the rewards on your self-reward menu to give yourself positive recognition or praise. An example might be buying yourself new shoes for eating less and exercising more. Display your self-reward menu in a highly-visible place on a colorful index card to increase your confidence.

Step One: List Desired New Behavior

New Behavior or Habit:

_____

Step Two: Make a List of Positive Self-Rewards

1. _____

2. _____

3. _____

4. _____

5. _____

Small Step Success Therapy

Identifying the gradual realistic steps involved in change can help people reach a goal. Breaking a large goal into small manageable steps increases people's confidence that they can change. Making progress on small steps reinforces positive behavioral change. Small victories can help people reach an important goal. Small step success therapy starts with a first step which motivates people to take the second and then the third and final committed step in the direction of valued change.

Describe a Change You are Considering:

_____

_____

List 3 Small Steps to Reach Your Goal

1. _____

2. _____

3. _____

Relaxation Training: Develop Good Breathing Habits

Relaxation training is one of the most effective ways to reduce anxiety and stress and to enhance health and wellness. Knowing how to relax can improve your health and performance and reduce chronic pain. Relaxation training includes learning new breathing habits, muscle relaxation, and imagery or visualizations.

Step One: Become More Mindful of How You Breath

Breathing correctly is essential to our health. The right balance of oxygen and discharge of carbon dioxide is essential for the mind and body to function. The muscles in the abdomen tighten in response to stress. As the result of stress and anxiety, oxygen that we do inhale remains high in the lungs. Chest breathing is unhealthy for both the mind and body as people use more muscle and get less oxygen. Irregular breathing also increases the physical symptoms of anxiety. To improve your breathing habits, begin to become more mindful of how you breathe.

Step Two: Practice Three-Minute Mindful Breathing

To learn deep cleansing abdominal breathing, place one hand on your chest and the other on your abdomen. Next breath in and out as you normally do and notice what happens to your hands on your chest and abdomen. With deep and relaxed abdominal breathing the hand on your chest should stay still, while the hand on your abdomen should move like a balloon is inflating under it when you inhale and deflating when you exhale. To practice mindful breathing, schedule a time to practice and relax everyday for 3 minutes. Sit or lie down and close your eyes. As you breathe, visualize a balloon inflating and deflating as you breathe deeper and feel more relaxed. Daily practice leads to better breathing habits. The habit of abdominal breathing improves health and reduces stress and anxiety.

Relaxation Training: Progressive Muscle Relaxation

Relaxation training is one of the most effective ways to reduce anxiety and stress and to enhance health and wellness. Knowing how to relax can improve your health and performance and reduce pain. Relaxation training includes learning new breathing habits, muscle relaxation, and imagery or visualizations.

Step One: Learn About Progressive Muscle Relaxation (PMR)

Intentionally tensing and then relaxing muscle groups in the body can produce a deep sense of relaxation. The four muscle groups in the body include the arms, head, midsection, and legs. After tensing and relaxing each muscle, it is important to feel the difference between tensed muscles and relaxation. Regular practice of progressive muscle relaxation can send powerful signals to the brain to RELAX.

Step Two: Brief Progressive Muscle Relaxation

Sit in a comfortable chair and visualize the muscle(s) you intend to tense and then relax. Unlike some highly-structured time-consuming PMR exercises, simply select muscles in your body that you feel are tense. In this brief PMR exercise, custom design your own program. Once you have identified the muscle, visualize the muscle and then squeeze and hold for about 5 seconds. After 5 seconds, quickly release and feel the difference between tension and relaxation. As an example, close and clench your fist and then release it. Use this same procedure with tense muscles in different areas of your body.

Step Three: Identify Muscles You Want to Relax

Right hand/forearm	Right upper arm	Left hand/forearm	Left upper arm
Forehead	Eyes and cheeks	Mouth and jaw	Neck
Shoulders	Shoulder blades	Chest and stomach	Hips and buttocks
Right upper leg	Right lower leg	Right foot	Left upper leg
Left lower leg	Left foot	Upper back	Lower back

Relaxation Training: Visualizations and Imagery

Relaxation training is one of the most effective ways to reduce anxiety and stress and to enhance health and wellness. Knowing how to relax can improve your health and performance and reduce pain. Relaxation training includes learning new breathing habits, muscle relaxation, and imagery or visualizations.

Step One:
Use Relaxation Imagery to Reduce Stress & Promote Healing

Actively imaging a pleasant scene like a warm sunny day on the beach or at a log cabin on a lake in the mountains can help to calm and soothe the mind and body. Relaxation imagery involves visualizing safe and peaceful scenes and vividly sensing sounds, smells, and feelings of actually being right there on the beach or on the shoreline of the peaceful lake. Imagery is not just a mental visualization technique, but a mind/body process that involves our imagination, senses, mind, spirit and body. Everyone has a favorite place where they go to relax and enjoy time away from the everyday hassles of life. The benefit of relaxation imagery is the mind believes that the visualization is real so it acts, senses, feels and remembers like it really is in the mountains, at the beach, or on a cruise. Visualization can be used to help you reduce stress and worry and increase inner peace and calm.

Step Two:
Script and Record Your Own Safe and Relaxing Scene

Spend time creating in words a vivid description of the peaceful scene where you love to go to relax. After creating your scene in words, devote time in your day to sit, relax and visualize your favorite place. You also may choose to record it on a tape recorder or CD in your own voice for your listening and relaxing pleasure.

Reduce Anxiety and Worry: Engage in Absorbing Activities

Engaging in satisfying activities and distraction are highly-effective ways to reduce symptoms of worry and anxiety. When people are feeling anxious, their minds are often racing with automatic, anxious thoughts and their bodies are experiencing overwhelming physical symptoms of anxiety. Helpful distraction techniques include becoming totally absorbed in an activity where we completely forget about our anxious thoughts, feelings, sensations, and memories. Prepare a list of your favorite hobbies or absorbing activities that you can do to distract yourself when you are dwelling or obsessing about someone or something. An example of an absorbing activity that requires concentration is gardening or going to watch a comedy which takes you mind off of worries.

List Your Favorite Absorbing Activities that Require Concentration

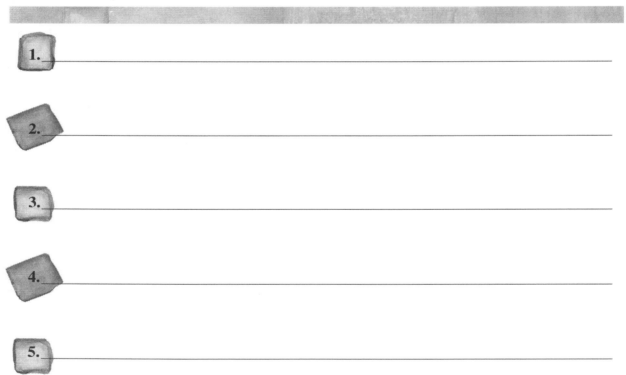

1. _____

2. _____

3. _____

4. _____

5. _____

Gradual Exposure to Feared Situations

One of the hallmarks of anxiety is avoidance. People actively avoid unpleasant people, anxious thoughts, painful memories and uncomfortable situations that activate anxiety and fears. Initially avoidance works because it provides a reduction in anxiety and relief from fear. In the long run however, avoidance can cause serious anxiety disorders and increases fears about facing certain people and situations. Safe gradual and continual exposure to fear eventually reduces the fear. Like diving into a cold lake or ocean eventually the body gets used to the temperature of the water. It is helpful when picking a situation or person that you have been avoiding, to select one that you truly need to stop avoiding. Ironically, facing your fears is the best way to overcome them.

List Situations You are Avoiding

1. _____

2. _____

3. _____

Step Two: Develop Safe and Gradual Steps

To overcome a feared situation or person, it is important to gradually expose yourself to the situation that is causing the anxiety. Make of list of steps beginning with the easiest smallest step working your way up to more difficult steps. While you will feel anxious, eventually this anxiety will melt away. You may choose to use some of the relaxation strategies to help you cope with the higher levels of anxiety you will experience when you complete your safe gradual exposure strategies.

Self-Affirmation Therapy

Positive self-affirmations are designed to strengthen positive self-statements and chip away at our strong negative inner core beliefs. It is normal to experience resistance when we challenge some of our long-held deeper negative beliefs. Short, powerful, positive statements are designed to increase wealth and success, improve physical health, heal emotional pain, and challenge self-defeating behaviors. Create your own personal self-affirmation index cards. Strategies to utilize the positive power of self-affirmation include: (a) say them while looking in the mirror, (b) read them out loud with feeling, (c) record your own affirmations, (d) write them down on index cards, (e) repeat them, silently or aloud, daily and (f) sing them to the tune of a favorite song.

I Am: Statements About Who You are

_____

_____

_____

I Can: Statements of Potential

_____

_____

_____

I Will: Statements of Positive Change

_____

_____

_____

Mindfulness Practices

When our brain is on *automatic pilot mode* we are often preoccupied and glued to our automatic negative thoughts about the past or future. In mindfulness practices, we discover the benefits of living in the moment, in the here and now, one day at a time.

With mindfulness we try to observe and notice new things and live more deeply in the present moment without judging experiences as good or bad. Instead of thinking, we switch to sensing and observing our mind, body, and experiences. Mindfulness practices help us to focus more on what is happening right now and less on what's going on inside our minds.

One way to practice mindfulness is to increase awareness while doing everyday routine activities. Listed below are some suggested activities where you can begin to practice moment-to-moment awareness. The purpose of the activities are to help you notice the difference between being in automatic pilot mode where your mind wanders and the being mode where you are fully present, enjoying the here and now. Try each activity and become more mindful of the difference between your automatic pilot brain that daydreams and wanders, and the soothing, calming feelings of enjoying each breath, each footstep, or each moment. Listed below are three activities where people can practice mindfulness by just noticing and observing while participating in the activities.

Increase Your Mindfulness Skills

Practice Three-Minute Mindful Breathing
Practice 10-Minute Mindful Walking
Practice Mindful Eating

Increase Positive Behaviors with Behavioral Contracts

Commitment and motivation are key to behavioral change. Initiating and maintaining change is easier when people make a written contract with themselves. These behavioral contracts are designed to help people put their decisions to change in writing. A contract helps people identify what behavior they want to change, when they want to start, the positive benefits of change, and strategies to deal with any stumbling blocks. Finally, the contract helps people anticipate the negative consequences of not following through with the steps outlined in the behavioral contract. Signing the contract implies that you have made a decision and agree with the contract.

Three-Month Behavioral Contract

Describe the Behavior You Wish to Change:
Date You Want to Begin:
List Expected Positive Benefits of Change:
List Anticipated Stumbling Blocks:
List Strategies to Overcome Stumbling Blocks:
List Negative Consequences if You do Not Complete the Contract:
Your Signature:_____Date:_____

Self-Monitoring Habits You Want to Modify or Change

In behavior therapy, one of the first steps is to become more aware of behaviors and habits that we want to change. One easy and effective suggestion is to record the behavior that people want to modify or change in a diary or journal. For each day, list if you engaged in the behaviors and others factors that you feel may have triggered the behavior.

Behavior to Monitor: _____

_____

Day of the Week	Frequency and Triggers of Behaviors
Monday:	
Tuesday:	
Wednesday:	
Thursday:	
Friday:	
Saturday:	
Sunday:	

Behavioral Activation:
Increase Pleasurable Activities

Developing a positive action plan can help you change habits and feel better. Increasing pleasurable activities is especially helpful for people who experience problems with depression. Listing positive steps will help to increase your confidence in the fact that you can change or improve. Increasing pleasurable activities increases your contact with positive reinforcement that helps build positive new habits.

Goal: Increase Pleasurable Activities

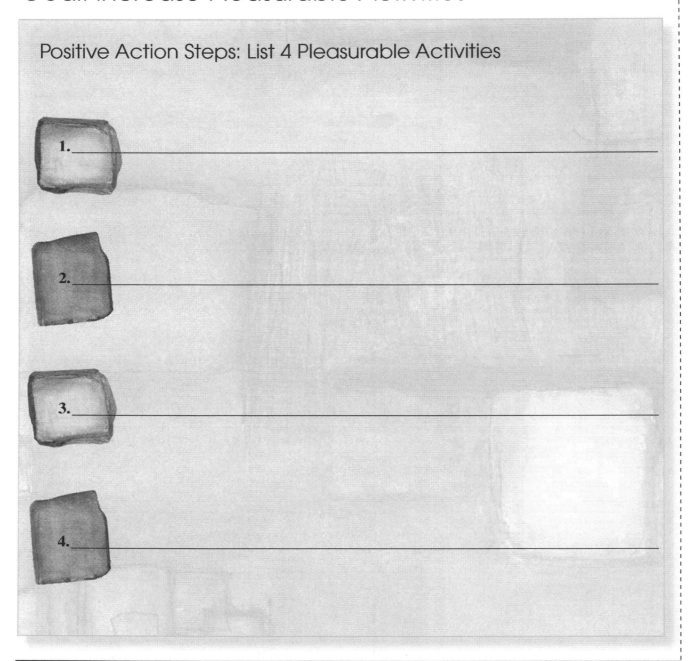

Positive Action Steps: List 4 Pleasurable Activities

1. _____

2. _____

3. _____

4. _____

Positive Action Plan: Act More Assertive

Assertiveness is the skill or ability to express your feelings, opinions and needs in a calm and clear manner without forcing them on others. Being assertive does not mean yelling and screaming or passively ignoring your own feelings and needs. Learning to be more assertive helps people stand up for themselves, solve problems, resolve conflicts, compromise, set boundaries, say no, express feelings, get needs met, and stop inappropriate behaviors. To learn how to be more assertive, list situations where you want to be more assertive and then create a list of steps you believe will help you be more assertive. Assertiveness is a skill and habit that is best learned with dedicated daily practice with everyday situations. Act as if you feel you are assertive.

Step One: Identify Situations Where You Need to Be More Assertive

1. _____

2. _____

3. _____

4. _____

Step Two: Identify Steps You Might Take to Act More Assertive

1. _____

2. _____

3. _____

4. _____

Positive Action Plan: Increase Self-Esteem

Self-esteem is a measure of how much you value or believe in yourself. Feeling like you are not important or having low self-esteem significantly impacts how people feel and what they do. People with low self-esteem act and feel as if they are not important. One helpful way to build self-esteem is to list eight positive qualities about yourself and then focus on these qualities when you are feeling upset or down. After listing 8 qualities, think of situations in your life where you do have good self-esteem.

Step One: List Eight Positive Qualities About Yourself

1. _____

2. _____

3. _____

4. _____

5. _____

6. _____

7. _____

8. _____

Positive Action Plan:
Reduce Procrastination

Developing a positive action plan can help you change habits and feel better. Listing positive steps will help to increase your confidence in the fact that you can change or improve. List 4 ways you can reduce procrastination.

Goal: Reduce Procrastination

Positive Action Steps: List 4 Ways to Reduce Procrastination

1. _____

2. _____

3. _____

4. _____

Positive Action Plan: Reduce Depression

Developing a positive action plan can help you change habits and feel better. Listing positive steps will help to increase your confidence in the fact that you can change or improve. List 4 ways you can reduce depression.

Goal: Reduce Depression

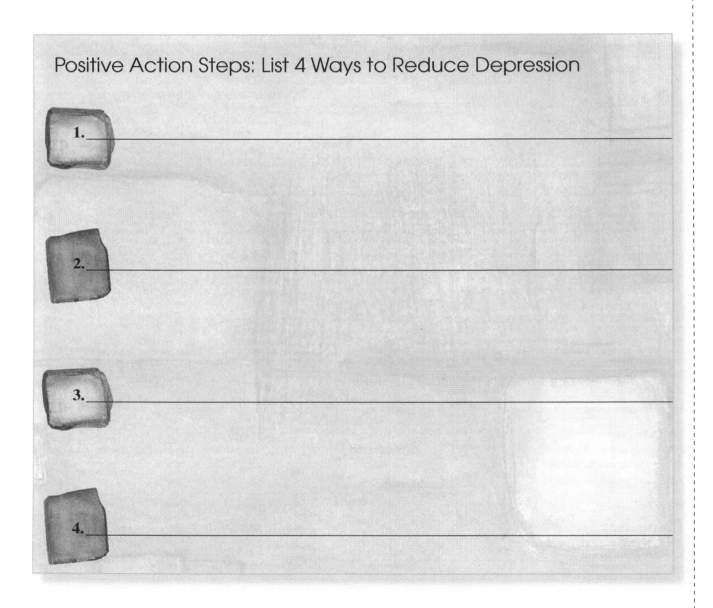

Positive Action Steps: List 4 Ways to Reduce Depression

1. _____

2. _____

3. _____

4. _____

Positive Action Plan:
Improve Medication Adherence

Developing a positive action plan can help you change habits and feel better. Listing positive steps will help to increase your confidence in the fact that you can change or improve. Taking medications as prescribed by your doctor for things like depression or cholesterol can dramatically improve how you feel and reduce negative symptoms. List 4 ways you can improve medication adherence.

Goal: Improve Medication Adherence

Positive Action Steps:
List 4 Ways to Improve Medication Adherence

1. _____

2. _____

3. _____

4. _____

Positive Action Plan: Reduce Anxiety

Developing a positive action plan can help you change habits and feel better. Listing positive steps will help to increase your confidence in the fact that you can change or improve. List 4 ways you can reduce anxiety.

Goal: Reduce Anxiety

Positive Action Steps: List 4 Ways to Reduce Anxiety

1. _____

2. _____

3. _____

4. _____

Positive Action Plan: Reduce High-Risk Drinking

Developing a positive action plan can help you change habits and feel better. Listing positive steps will help to increase your confidence in the fact that you can change or improve. List 4 ways you can reduce high-risk drinking habits.

Goal: Reduce High-Risk Drinking

Positive Action Steps: List 4 Ways to Reduce High-Risk Drinking

1. _____

2. _____

3. _____

4. _____

Positive Action Plan: Reduce Relationship Problems

Developing a positive action plan can help you change habits and feel better. Listing positive steps will help to increase your confidence in the fact that you can change or improve. List 4 ways you can reduce relationship problems.

Goal: Reduce Relationship Problems

Positive Action Steps:
List 4 Ways to Reduce Relationship Problems

1. _____

2. _____

3. _____

4. _____

Positive Action Plan: Reduce Guilt and Shame

Developing a positive action plan can help you change habits and feel better. Listing positive steps will help to increase your confidence in the fact that you can change or improve. List 4 ways you can reduce guilt and shame.

Goal: Reduce Guilt/Shame

Positive Action Steps: List 4 Ways to Reduce Guilt/Shame

1. _____

2. _____

3. _____

4. _____

Positive Action Plan: Anger Management Strategies

Developing a positive action plan can help you change habits and feel better. Listing positive steps will help to increase your confidence in the fact that you can change or improve. List 4 ways you can manage anger.

Goal: Anger Management Strategies

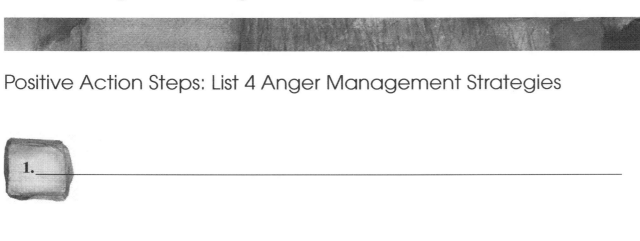

Positive Action Steps: List 4 Anger Management Strategies

1. _____

2. _____

3. _____

4. _____

Positive Action Plan: Increase Social Supports

Developing a positive action plan can help you change habits and feel better. Listing positive steps will help to increase your confidence in the fact that you can change or improve. List 4 ways you can increase your social supports.

Goal: Increase Social Supports

Positive Action Steps: List 4 Ways to Increase Social Supports

 1. _____

 2. _____

 3. _____

 4. _____

Positive Action Plan: Reduce Feelings of Inferiority

Developing a positive action plan can help you change habits and feel better. Listing positive steps will help to increase your confidence in the fact that you can change or improve. List 4 ways you can reduce feelings of inferiority.

Goal: Reduce Feelings of Inferiority

Positive Action Steps: List 4 Ways to Reduce Feelings of Inferiority

1. _____

2. _____

3. _____

4. _____

Positive Action Plan: Reduce Avoidance

Developing a positive action plan can help you change habits and feel better. Listing positive steps will help to increase your confidence in the fact that you can change or improve. List 4 ways you can reduce avoidance.

Goal: Reduce Avoidance

Positive Action Steps: List 4 Ways to Reduce Avoidance

 1. _____

 2. _____

 3. _____

 4. _____

Positive Action Plan: Manage Stress

Developing a positive action plan can help you change habits and feel better. Listing positive steps will help to increase your confidence in the fact that you can change or improve. List 4 ways you can reduce and manage stress.

Goal: Manage Stress

Positive Action Steps: List 4 Ways to Manage Stress

1. _____

2. _____

3. _____

4. _____

Positive Action Plan: Increase Physical Activity

Increasing physical activity will enhance both your physical and mental health. Physical activity like exercise, are great for the mind and body. One of the best ways to prevent serious health problems is to increase daily physical activity.

Goal: Increase Physical Activity

Positive Action Steps: List 4 Ways to Increase Physical Activity

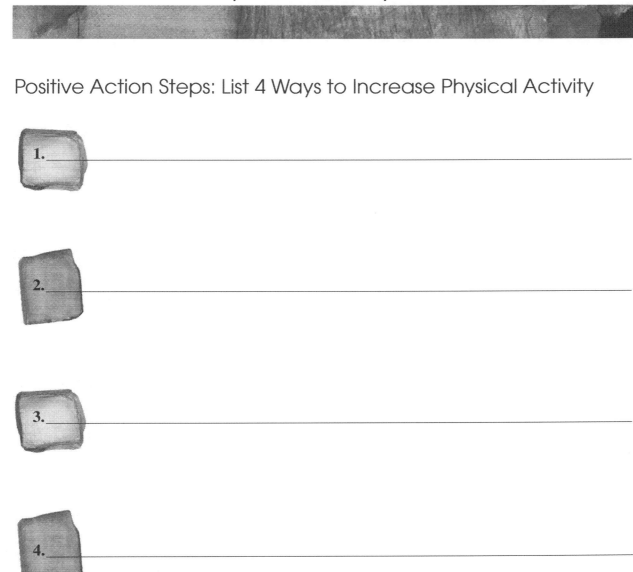

1. _____

2. _____

3. _____

4. _____

Positive Action Plan: Improve Eating Habits

Developing a positive action plan can help you change habits and feel better. Listing positive steps will help to increase your confidence in the fact that you can change or improve. List 4 ways you can improve your eating habits.

Goal: Improve Eating Habits

Positive Action Steps: List 4 Ways to Improve Eating Habits

1. _____

2. _____

3. _____

4. _____

Positive Action Plan: Lose Weight

Developing a positive action plan can help you change habits and feel better. Listing positive steps will help to increase your confidence in the fact that you can change or improve. List 4 ways you can lose weight.

Goal: Lose Weight

Positive Action Steps: List 4 Ways to Lose Weight

 1. _____

 2. _____

 3. _____

 4. _____

Positive Action Plan: Increase Exercise

Developing a positive action plan can help you change habits and feel better. Listing positive steps will help to increase your confidence in the fact that you can change or improve. List 4 ways you can increase your exercise.

Goal: Increase Exercise

Positive Action Steps: List 4 Ways to Increase Exercise

1. _____

2. _____

3. _____

4. _____

Positive Action Plan: Improve Sleeping Habits

Developing a positive action plan can help you change habits and feel better. Listing positive steps will help to increase your confidence in the fact that you can change or improve. List 4 ways you can improve your sleeping habits.

Goal: Improve Sleeping Habits

Positive Action Steps: List 4 Ways to Improve Sleeping Habits

 1. _____

 2. _____

 3. _____

 4. _____

Positive Action Plan: Improve Parenting Practices

Developing a positive action plan can help you change habits and feel better. Listing positive steps will help to increase your confidence in the fact that you can change or improve. List 4 ways you can improve your parenting practices.

Goal: Improve Parenting Practices

Positive Action Steps: List 4 Ways to Improve Parenting Practices

1. _____

2. _____

3. _____

4. _____

Positive Action Plan:
Improve Intimate Relationships

Developing a positive action plan can help you change habits and feel better. Listing positive steps will help to increase your confidence in the fact that you can change or improve. List 4 ways you can improve your intimate relationships.

Goal: Improve Intimate Relationships

Positive Action Steps:
List 4 Ways to Improve Intimate Relationships

1.

2.

3.

4.

Positive Action Plan: Improve Family Relationships

Developing a positive action plan can help you change habits and feel better. Listing positive steps will help to increase your confidence in the fact that you can change or improve. List 4 ways you can improve your family relationships.

Goal: Improve Family Relationships

Positive Action Steps: List 4 Ways to Improve Family Relationships

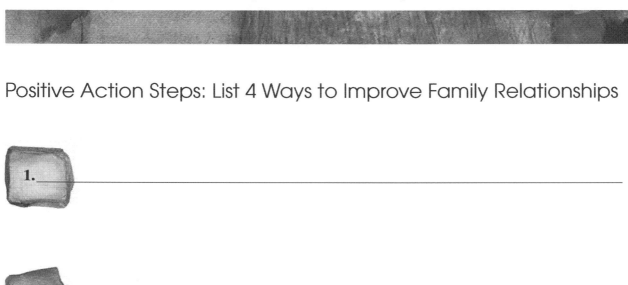

1. _____

2. _____

3. _____

4. _____

Positive Action Plan: Improve Social Skills

Developing a positive action plan can help you change habits and feel better. Listing positive steps will help to increase your confidence in the fact that you can change or improve. List 4 ways you can improve your social skills or interpersonal skills in relationships.

Goal: Improve Social Skills in Relationships

Positive Action Steps: List 4 Ways to Improve Social Skills

1. _____

2. _____

3. _____

4. _____

Positive Action Plan:
Increase Positive Coping Skills

Developing a positive action plan can help you change habits and feel better. Listing positive steps will help to increase your confidence in the fact that you can change or improve. Frequently when we face challenges, problems, and stress we learn good and not-so-good ways of coping with these situations. Increasing positive coping skills is helpful for most of life's toughest challenges.

Goal: Increase Positive Coping Skills

Positive Action Steps: List 4 Positive Coping Skills

1. _____

2. _____

3. _____

4. _____

Positive Action Plan:
Cope with Memories of Trauma

Developing a positive action plan can help you learn how to cope with difficult situations and unpleasant memories. Listing positive steps will help to increase your confidence in the fact that you can learn to cope with traumatic memories and unpleasant feelings. Your ideas are probably the best, as only you feel what is right for you. List 4 ways that can help you cope with some of the painful memories and feelings you still have related to any past trauma.

Goal: Cope with Memories of Trauma

Positive Action Steps:
List 4 Ways to Cope with Memories of Trauma

1. _____

2. _____

3. _____

4. _____

Positive Action Plan: Cope with Grief and Loss

Losing someone can be very painful. People experiencing grief and loss are frequently overwhelmed with a wide range of feelings including shock, anger and guilt. Adjusting to loss is never easy and no one can tell someone how they should cope with their personal grief and loss. The purpose of this exercise is to help people develop a personalized plan for coping with grief and loss. Coping can include getting support from friends and family, turning to spiritual support systems, taking good care of yourself, and/or seeing a professional mental health counselor trained in grief counseling. List some coping strategies that you feel could help you to cope with your feelings of grief and loss.

Goal: Cope with Grief and Loss

Positive Action Strategies: List Ways to Cope with Grief and Loss

1. _____

2. _____

3. _____

4. _____

Source: Helpguide.org. A Trusted Non-Profit Resource

Relapse Prevention: Identify Relapse Warning Signs

Like a cross-country road trip, recovery has many detours, rough terrains and slippery roads. Recognizing and anticipating warning signs can help alert you to the potential dangers of relapse. Like a fire alarm before the actual fire, early recognition can help you take steps that prevent serious harm. Warning signs can include high-risk situations like negative emotional states, social pressures, relationship conflicts, urges and temptations, and peers. When thinking about a behavior that you trying to change, list the warning signs or situations that trigger the behavior. After identifying these triggers, think about ways that you can avoid or cope with these high-risk situations. High-risk situations can also include situations in the past when you did slip or lapse. One of the best ways to avoid relapse is to avoid the trigger that causes the slip or lapse. Also, if you do slip, use it as a learning opportunity to help you in your recovery.

Identify 4 Relapse Warning Signs

1. _____

2. _____

3. _____

4. _____

Source: Dr. G. Allan Marlatt, *Relapse Prevention*

Relapse Prevention: Recovery Support Plan

Maintaining long-term recovery with addiction and mental health disorders requires building a strong support system and a recovery support plan. A plan includes working to develop a positive network of people, self-help meetings, pleasant activities, and a balanced lifestyle. Taking needed medications, getting support from a mental health professional and attending faith-based support organizations can all be a part of a recovery support plan. The best plan is the one that works for you. Make a list of four of the most important items in your recovery support plan and consider putting them on index cards for visual and daily review.

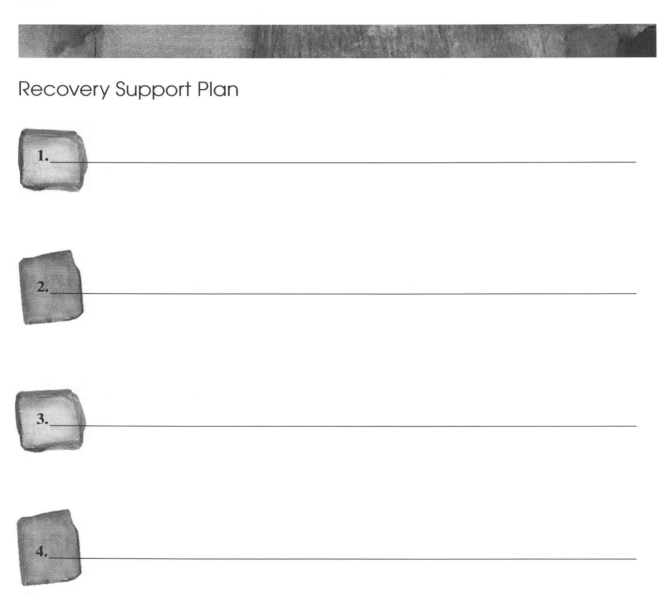

Recovery Support Plan

1. _____

2. _____

3. _____

4. _____

References

Amen, D. G. (1998). *Change your brain, change your life*. New York: Three Rivers Press.

Amen, D. G. *Images of human behavior: A brain spect atlas*. Retrieved July 8, 2008 from http://amenclinics.com/bp/atlas/

Arkowitz, H., Westra, H. A., Miller, W. R., & Rollnick, S. (Eds). (2008). *Motivational interviewing in the treatment of psychological problems*. New York: The Guilford Press.

Amen, D. G. (1996). *Change your brain, change your life*. New York: Three River Press.

Beck, A. T., & Emery, G., & Greenberg, R. (1985). *Anxiety disorders and phobias: A cognitive perspective*. New York: Basic Books.

Beck, A. T. (1988). *Love is never enough: How couples can overcome misunderstandings, resolve conflicts, and solve relationship problems through cognitive therapy*. New York: Harper & Row.

Beck, A. T., (1976). *Cognitive therapy and the emotional disorders*. New York: Penguin Group.

Beck, A. T., Wright, F. D., Newman, C. F., & Liese, B. S. (1993). *Cognitive therapy of substance abuse*. New York: The Guilford Press.

Beck, A. T., Freeman, A., Davis, D. D., & Associates. (2004). *Cognitive therapy of personality disorders* (2nd Ed.). New York: The Guilford Press.

Beck, A. T., Rush, A. J., Shaw, B. F., & Emery, G. (1979). *Cognitive therapy of depression*. New York: The Guilford Press.

Beck, J. S. (1995). *Cognitive therapy: Basics and beyond*. New York: The Guilford Press.

Beck, J. S. (2005). *Cognitive therapy for challenging problems*. New York: The Guilford Press.

Beck, J. S. (2007). *The Beck diet solution: Train your brain to think like a thin person*. Alabama: Oxmoor House, Inc.

Begley, S. (2008). *Train your mind, change your brain*. New York: Ballantine Books.

Bernard, M. E., & Wolfe, J. L. (Eds). (2000). *The RET resource book for practitioners*. New York: The Institute for Rational-Emotive Therapy.

Branch, R., & Wilson, R. (2007). *Cognitive behavioural therapy for dummies*. England: John Wiley & Sons, Ltd.

Burns, D. D. (1999). *Feeling good: The new mood therapy* (Rev. ed.). New York: Avon Books.

Burns, D. D. (1989). *The feeling good handbook*. New York: Plume.

Butler, A. C., Chapman, J. E., Forman, E. M., & Beck, A. T. (2006). *The empirical status of cognitive-behavioral therapy: A review of meta-analyses*. Clinical Psychology Review, 26, 17-31.

Center for Substance Abuse Treatment. (1999). *Enhancing motivation to change in substance abuse treatment*. Treatment Improvement Protocol Series (TIPS). DHHS Pub. No. (SMA) 99-3354. Washington, D.C: U.S. Government Printing Office.

Center for Substance Abuse Treatment. (1999). *Brief interventions and brief therapies for substance abuse.* Treatment Improvement Protocol Series (TIPS). DHHS Pub. No. (SMA) 99-3353. Washington, D.C: U.S. Government Printing Office.

Corey, G. (2005). *Theory and practice of counseling and psychotherapy.* California: Thomson Brooks/Cole.

Cozolino, L. (2002). *The neuroscience of psychotherapy.* New York: W.W. Norton & Company, Inc.

Carroll, K. M. (1998). *A cognitive-behavioral approach: Treating cocaine addiction.* Rockville, Maryland, National Institute on Drug Abuse. Therapy Manual for Drug Addiction. U. S. Department of Health and Human Services.

Daley, D. C., & Marlatt, G. A. (2006). *Overcoming your alcohol or drug problem: effective recovery strategies workbook.* New York: Oxford University Press, Inc.

Davis, M., Eshelman, E. R., & McKay, M. (1995). *The relaxation & stress reduction workbook.* California: New Harbinger Publications, Inc.

Deblinger, E., Kolar, R. T. & Ryan, E. Trauma in Childhood. In Follette, V. M., & Ruzek, J. I. (Eds.). *Cognitive-behavioral therapies for trauma* (pp. 405-432). New York: The Guilford Press.

Dimidjian, S., Dobson, K. S., Kohlenberg, R. J., Gallop, R., Markley, D. K., Atkins, D. C., et al. (2006). Randomized trial of behavioral activation, cognitive therapy, and antidepressant medication in the acute treatment of adults with major depression. *Journal of Consulting and Clinical Psychology*, 74, 658-670.

Gregory, B. (2004). *The college success workbook: Promoting student success inside & outside the classroom.* Boynton Beach: Life Skills Publishing Co.

Greenberger, D., & Padesky, C. A. (1995). *Mind over mood.* New York: The Guilford Press.

Foa, E. B., Rothbaum, B. O., Riggs, D. S., & Murdock, T. B. (1991). Treatment of posttraumatic stress disorder in rape victims: A comparison between cognitive-behavioral procedures and counseling. *Journal of Consulting and Clinical Psychology.* 59(5), 715-723.

Freeman, A., Felgoise, H. S., Nezu, A. M., Nezu, M. C., & Reinecke, M. A. (Eds). (2005). *Encyclopedia of cognitive behavior therapy,* New York: Springer.

Freeman, A., Pretzer, J., Fleming, B., & Simon, K. M. (2004). *Clinical applications of cognitive therapy* (2nd ed.). New York: Kluwer Academic/Plenum Publishers.

Goodheart, C. D., Kazdin, A. E., & Sternberg, R. J. (Eds). (2006). *Evidence-based psychotherapy.* Washington, D.C.: American Psychological Association.

Harris, R. (2006). Embracing your demons: An overview of acceptance and commitment therapy. *Psychotherapy in Australia*, 12, pp. 2-8.

Hester, R. K., & Miller, W.R. (2003). *Handbook of alcoholism treatment approaches: Effective alternatives.* Needham Heights, MA: Allyn & Bacon.

Higgins, S. T., & Petry N. M. (1999). Contingency Management: Incentives for Sobriety. *Alcohol Research and Health*, 23(2):122-127.

Higgins, S. T., Budney, A. J., Bickel, W. K.. Hughes, J. R., Foerg, F., & Badger, G. (1993). Achieving cocaine abstinence with a behavioral approach. *American Journal of Psychiatry*, 150(5): 763-769..

Higgins, S. T., Tidey, J. W., & Stizer, M. L. (1998). Community reinforcement and contingency management interventions. In: Graham, A.W.: Schultz, T.K.: and Wilford, B.B. (Eds.) *Principles of Addiction Medicine* (2d ed.) (pp. 675-690).Chevy Chase, MD: American Society of Addiction Medicine, Inc.

Hinshaw, S. P. Attention-deficit/hyperactivity disorder: The search for viable treatments. In Kendall, P.C. (Ed.). *Child and Adolescent Therapy Cognitive-Behavioral Procedures* (pp. 88-128). New York: The Guilford Press.

Hunt, G.M., & Azrin, N.H. (1973). A community reinforcement approach to alcoholism. *Behavior Research and Therapy*, 11, 91-104.

Huss, D. B., & Baer, R. A. (2007). Acceptance and change: The integration of mindfulness-based cognitive therapy into ongoing dialectical behavior therapy in a case of borderline personality disorder with depression. *Clinical Case Studies*, 6(1), 17-33.

Institute of Medicine. (2001). *Crossing the quality chasm: A new health system for the 21st century.* Washington, DC: National Academies Press.

Jacobson, N. S., & Christensen, A. (1998). *Acceptance and change in couples therapy: A therapist's guide to transforming relationships.* New York: W. W. Norton & Company.

Jacobson, N. S., Martell, C. R., & Dimidjian, S. (2001). Behavioral activation treatment for depression: Returning to contextual roots. *Clinical Psychology: Science and Practice*, 8, 255-270.

Kadden, R., Carroll, K. M., Donovan, D., Cooney, N., Monti, P., Abrams, D., et al. (2002). *Cognitive-behavioral coping skills therapy manual: A clinical research guide for therapists treating individuals with alcohol abuse and dependence.* NIAAA Project Match Monograph Series Vol. 3 DHHS Pub. No. (ADM) 92-1895. Rockville, MD: National Institute on Alcohol Abuse and Alcoholism.

Kendall, P. C. (Ed). (2000). *Child and adolescent therapy: Cognitive-behavioral procedures.* New York: The Guilford Press.

Kendall, P. C., Chu, B. C., Pimentel, S. S., & Choudhury, M. (2000). Treating anxiety disorders in youth. In Kendall, P.C. (Ed). *Child and adolescent therapy: Cognitive-behavioral procedures* (pp. 235-287). New York: The Guilford Press.

Kohlenberg, B. S., Tsai, M., & Kohlenberg, R. J. (1998). Functional analytic psychotherapy and the treatment of complex posttraumatic stress disorder. In Follette, V. M., & Ruzek, J. I. (Eds.). *Cognitive-behavioral therapies for trauma* (pp. 173-200). New York: The Guilford Press.

Kubany, E. S., & Ralston, R. C. (1998). Cognitive Therapy for Trauma-Related Guilt and Shame. In Follette, V. M., & Ruzek, J. I. (Eds.). *Cognitive-behavioral therapies for trauma* (pp. 258-289). New York: The Guilford Press.

Lambert, M. J. (1992). Psychotherapy outcome research: Implications for integrative and eclectic therapists. In J. C. Norcross (Ed.). *Handbook of psychotherapy integration* (pp. 436-462). New York: Brunner/Mazel.

Lambert, M. J., & Barley, D. E. (2002). Research summary on the therapeutic relationship and psychotherapy outcome. In J. C. Norcross (Ed.). *Psychotherapy relationships that work: Therapist contributions and responsiveness to patients* (pp. 17-32). New York: Oxford University Press.

Langelier, C. A., & Connell, J. D. (2005). Emotions and learning: Where brain based research and cognitive-behavioral counseling strategies meet the road. *Rivier College Online Academic Journal*, 1, Fall, 1-13.

Leahy, R. L. (2003). *Cognitive therapy techniques: A practitioner's guide.* New York: The Guilford Press.

Leonard, L. M., Follette, V. M., & Compton, J. S. (2006). A principle-based intervention for couples affected by trauma. In Follette, V. M., & Ruzek, J. I. (Eds). *Cognitive-behavioral therapies for trauma* (pp. 362-387). New York: The Guilford Press.

Linehan, M. M. (1993a). *Cognitive-behavioral treatment of borderline personality disorder.* New York: The Guilford Press.

Linehan, M. M. (1993b). *Cognitive-behavioral treatment of borderline personality disorder*. New York: The Guilford Press

Lochman, J. E., Whidby, J. M., & FitzGerald, D. P. (2000). Cognitive-behavioral assessment and treatment with aggressive children. In Kendall, P.C. (Ed). *Child and adolescent therapy: Cognitive-behavioral procedures* (pp. 31-87). New York: The Guilford Press.

Longabaugh, R., & Morgenstern, J. (1999). Cognitive-behavioral coping-skills therapy for alcohol dependence: Current status and future direction. *Alcohol Research and Health*, 23(2):78-86.

Luoma, J. B., Hayes, S. C., & Walser, R. D. (2007). *Learning ACT: An acceptance & commitment therapy skills-training manual for therapists*. California: New Harbinger Publications, Inc.

Marlatt, G. A., & Gordon, J. R. (Eds). (2005). *Relapse prevention: Maintenance strategies in the treatment of addictive behaviors*. New York: The Guilford Press.

Marlatt, G. A., & Kristeller, J. (1999). Mindfulness and mediation. In W. R. Miller (Ed.). *Integating spirituality into treatment: Resources for practitioners* (pp. 67-84). Washington, D. C.: American Psychological Association Books.

Matsakis, A. (1996). *I can't get over it: A handbook for trauma survivors* (2nd ed.). California: New Harbinger Publications.

McKay, M., Davis, M., & Fanning, P. (1997). *Thoughts & feelings: Taking control of your moods and your life*. California: New Harbinger Publications.

McKay, M., Wood, J. C., & Brantley, J. (2007). *The dialectical behavior therapy skills workbook: Practical DBT exercises for learning mindfulness, interpersonal effectiveness, emotion regulation & distress tolerance*. (2007). California: New Harbinger Publications.

Meichenbaum, D. (1977). *Cognitive-behavior modification: An integrative approach*. New York: Springer.

Meichenbaum, D. (1985). *Stress inoculation training*. Boston, MA: Allyn & Bacon.

Meichenbaum, D. (1994). *A clinical handbook/practical therapist manual for assessing and treating adults with posttraumatic stress disorder (PTSD)*. Waterloo, Ontario: Institute Press.

Miller, W. R., Meyers, R. J., & Hiller-Sturmhöfel, S. (1999). The Community-Reinforcement Approach. *Alcohol Research and Health*, 23(2):116-121.

Hester, R. K., & Miller, W. R. (Eds). (2003). *Handbook of alcoholism treatment approaches*. Boston, MA: Allyn & Bacon.

Miller, W. R., & Rollnick, S. (1991). *Motivational interviewing: Preparing people for change*. New York: The Guilford Press.

Miller, W. R., & Rollnick, S. (2002). *Motivational interviewing: Preparing people for change*. New York: The Guilford Press.

Miller, W. R. (1995). *Motivational enhancement therapy with drug abusers*. Unpublished Therapist Manuscript: National Institute on Drug Abuse. Online: http://casaa.unm.edu/download/METManual.pdf

Miklowitz, D. J. (2002). Family-focused treatment for bipolar disorder. In Hofmann, S. G., & Tompson, M. C. (Ed), *Treating chronic and severe mental disorders: A handbook of empirically supported interventions* (pp. 159-174). New York: The Guilford Press.

Monti, P. M., Kadden, R. M., Rohsenow, D. J., Abrams, D. B., & Cooney, N. L. (1989). *Treating alcohol dependence: A coping skills training guide*. New York: The Guilford Press.

Monti, P. M., and Rohsehow, D. J. (1999). Coping-Skills Training and Cue-Exposure Therapy in the Treatment of Alcoholism. *Alcohol Research and Health*, 23(2):107-115.

Morgan, B., & Macmillan, P. (1999). Helping clients move toward constructive change: A three- phase integrative counseling model. *Journal of Counseling and Development*, 77(2), 153-159.

Najavits, L. M. (2006). Seeking Safety: Therapy for Posttraumatic Stress Disorder and Substance Use Disorder. In Follette, V. M., & Ruzek, J. I. (Eds.). *Cognitive-behavioral therapies for trauma* (pp. 228-257). New York: The Guilford Press.

Nock, M. K., & Mendes, W. B. (2008). Physiological arousal, distress tolerance, and social problem-solving deficits among adolescent self-injurers. *Journal of Consulting and Clinical Psychology*, 76(1), 28-38.

Padesky, C. A., & Greenberger, D. (1995). *Clinician's guide to mind over mood*. New York: The Guilford Press.

Padesky, C. A., & Greenberger, D. (1995). *Mind over mood*. New York: The Guilford Press.

Pucci, A. R. (2006). *The client's guide to cognitive-behavioral therapy: How to live a healthy, happy life...No matter what*. New York: iUniverse, Inc.

Resick, P. A., Nishith, P., Weaver, T. L., Astin, M. C., & Feuer, C. A. (2002). A comparison of cognitive-processing therapy with prolonged exposure and a waiting condition for the treatment of chronic posttraumatic stress disorder in female rape victims. *Journal of Consulting and Clinical Psychology*, 70(4), 867-879.

Riggs, D. S., Cahill, S. P., & Foa, E. B. (2006). Prolonged Exposure Treatment of Posttraumatic Stress Disorders. In Follette, V. M., & Ruzek, J. I. (Eds.), *Cognitive-behavioral therapies for trauma* (pp. 65-95). New York: The Guilford Press.

Segal, Z. V., Williams, J. M. G., & Teasdale, J. D. (2002). *Mindfulness-based cognitive therapy for depression*. New York: The Guilford Press.

Shapiro, F., & Maxfield, L. (2003). EMDR and information processing in psychotherapy treatment: personal development and global implications. In Solomon, M. F., & Siegel, D. J. (Eds.). *Healing Trauma: Attachment, mind, body, and brain* (pp. 196-220). New York: W. W. Norton & Company.

Shipherd, J. C., Street, A. E., & Resick, P. A. Cognitive Therapy for Posttraumatic Stress Disorder. In Follette, V. M., & Ruzek, J. I. (Eds.), *Cognitive-behavioral therapies for trauma* (pp. 96-116). New York: The Guilford Press.

Siegel, D. J. (2007). *The mindful brain: Reflection and attunement in the cultivation of well-being*. New York: W. W. Norton & Company.

Smith, J. E., Meyers, R. J., & Milford, J. L. (2003). What works? A summary of alcohol treatment outcome research. In Hester, R. K., & Miller, W. R. (Eds.). *Handbook of alcoholism treatment approaches* (pp. 237-258). Boston, MA: Allyn & Bacon.

Smucker, M. R., Dancu, C., Foa, E. B., & Niederee, J. L. (1995). Imagery rescripting: A new treatment for survivors of childhood sexual abuse suffering from posttraumatic stress. *Journal of Cognitive Psychotherapy: An International Quarterly*, 9(1), 3-17.

Solomon, M. F., & Siegel, D. J. (Eds). (2003). *Healing trauma: Attachment, mind, body, and brain*. New York: W. W. Norton & Company.

Sperry, L., Carlson, J., & Kjos, D. (2002). *Becoming an effective therapist*. Boston, MA: Allyn & Bacon.

Spiegler, M.D., & Guevremont, D.C. (2003). *Contemporary behavior therapy* (4th ed.). Belmont, CA: Wadsworth, Cengage Learning.

Stallard, P. (2002). *Think good-feel good: A cognitive behaviour therapy workbook for children and young people*. England: John Wiley & Sons, Ltd.

Stark, K. D., Sander, J. B., Yancy, M. G., Bronik, M. D., & Hoke, J. A. (2000). Treatment of depression in childhood and adolescence: Cognitvie-behavioral procedures for individual and family. In Kendall, P.C. (Ed). *Child and adolescent therapy: Cognitive-behavioral procedures* (2nd ed., pp. 173-234). New York: The Guilford Press.

Van der Kolk, B. A. (2003). Posttraumatic Stress Disorder and the nature of trauma. In Solomon, M. F., & Siegel, D. J. (Eds.). *Healing trauma: Attachment, mind, body, and brain* (pp. 168-195). New York: W. W. Norton & Company, Inc.

Young, J. E., & Klosko, J. S. (1993). *Reinventing Your Life: The breakthrough program to end negative behavior...and feel great again*. New York: Plume Books.

Young, J. E., Klosko, J. S., & Weishaar, M. E. (2003). *Schema therapy: A practitioner's guide*. New York: The Guilford Press.

Wagner, A. W., & Linehan, M. M. (2006). Applications of Dialectical Behavioral Therapy to Posttraumatic Stress Disorder and Related Problems. In Follette, V. M., & Ruzek, J. I. (Eds.), *Cognitive-behavioral therapies for trauma*. (pp. 117-145). New York: The Guilford Press.

Walser, R. D., & Hayes, S. C. Acceptance and Commitment Therapy in the Treatment of Postraumatic Stress Disorder: Theoretical and Applied Issues. In Follette, V. M., & Ruzek, J. I. (Eds.), *Cognitive-behavioral therapies for trauma* (pp. 146- 172). New York: The Guilford Press.

Wild, J., Hackman, A., & Clark, D. M. (2008). Rescripting early memories linked to negative images in social phobia: A pilot study. *Behavior Therapy*, 39(1), 47-56.

Williams, M., Teasdale, J., Segal, Z., & Kabat-Zinn, J. (2007). *The mindful way through depression: Freeing yourself from chronic unhappiness*. New York: The Guilford Press.

Personal Notes and Reflections

Personal Notes and Reflections

Made in the USA
San Bernardino, CA
26 November 2016

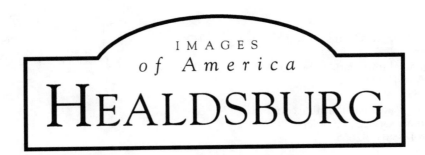

IMAGES
of America
HEALDSBURG

Healdsburg Museum and Historical Society

ARCADIA
PUBLISHING

Published by Arcadia Publishing
Charleston, South Carolina

Library of Congress Catalog Card Number: 2005929619

For all general information contact Arcadia Publishing at:
Telephone 843-853-2070
Fax 843-853-0044
E-mail sales@arcadiapublishing.com
For customer service and orders:
Toll-Free 1-888-313-2665

Visit us on the Internet at www.arcadiapublishing.com

The Russian River at Healdsburg is pictured in 1916 beside Fitch Mountain.

CONTENTS

Acknowledgments   6

Introduction   7

1.   First People   9

2.   Brave Old Days   17

3.   Builders of Our Heritage   25

4.   Intent on Learning   37

5.   Joyful Pursuits   49

6.   Churchgoing Folk   63

7.   Champions among Us   71

8.   Abundance and Enterprise   83

9.   Grapes in Profusion   97

10.   Calamities and Rejoicing   107

Surname Index   126

About the Healdsburg Museum   128

ACKNOWLEDGMENTS

This book would not have been possible without the volunteer effort of the many members of our community dedicated to the preservation and dissemination of the history of Healdsburg. Our contributors relied on museum archives, which contain a wealth of photographs, newspapers, records, and oral histories. They also received help from residents and others who generously shared their images. The book covers the first 100 years of our hometown's history.

We extend our appreciation to past president Bob Rawlins, who secured the original approval of the board of directors for the book project and has provided continuing assistance. Members of the publishing team include the following:

Elizabeth Holmes, image editor

Keith Power, text editor

Holly Hoods, research curator

Daniel F. Murley, curator

Charlotte Anderson and June Maher Smith, chief contributors

Anna Darden, Pat Keadle, Kay Robinson, Arnold Santucci, Sherrie Smith-Ferri, contributors

Pres. Al Loebel, administration and technical support

All images in this book, except as noted, are the property of the museum.

—Board of Directors
Healdsburg Museum and Historical Society

INTRODUCTION

The story of Healdsburg may be traced to a romance that began in the early 19th century.

Yankee sea captain Henry Fitch was a trader along the coast of California when it was under Spanish colonial rule and after Mexico's independence in 1821, when it became Mexican territory. In 1826, the dashing captain met Josefa Carrillo in San Diego. They fell in love but were denied permission to marry. The couple eloped, and ultimately their marriage was recognized. About 1844, Fitch, awarded Mexican citizenship in 1833, obtained a large land grant in what is now Sonoma County. He called it Rancho Sotoyome. During this Spanish-Mexican period, ranchos on the sparsely populated land raised cattle to produce hide and tallow as trading goods.

In 1846, war broke out between the United States and Mexico over a border dispute. The war ended in 1848 with the Treaty of Guadalupe-Hidalgo, which ceded California to the United States and guaranteed former Mexican citizens rights to property they held before the hostilities. A board of land commissioners was established in 1851 to judge the validity of Mexican land grants in the new State of California. In 1849, Fitch died in San Diego. His widow, Josefa Carrillo Fitch, and her nine children moved north to Rancho Sotoyome. She applied to the board for recognition of Fitch's land grant.

Meanwhile, the discovery of gold in California in 1848 provoked a wild scramble of prospectors into the Sierra foothills. Harmon Heald and his two brothers crossed the plains with thousands of other gold seekers and, like most of them, were disappointed at the diggings. Many of the newcomers settled without permission on land whose ownership was in dispute. Squatters invaded the Rancho Sotoyome and some required eviction later.

Heald built a cabin and a store on the site of what is now Healdsburg. The widow Fitch was declared in rightful possession of the rancho, but legal expenses and other debts forced her to auction off portions of the land. Heald bought the property and laid out the town's Plaza and its surrounding streets. In 1857, he filed a plat map of Healdsburg with county authorities, and 10 years later, the town was incorporated.

The story of the original inhabitants of the land involves going back in time thousands of years. The first chapter of this book introduces these resourceful people.

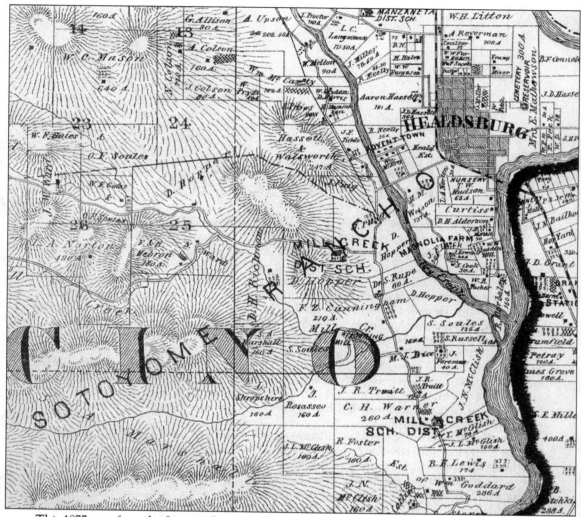

This 1877 map from the *Sonoma County Atlas* shows the major landowners and landmarks in the Healdsburg area between Litton (Lytton) Springs and Eastside Road. In addition to the locations of former one-room schoolhouses, the 1877 map shows that Healdsburg had a large Seventh-day Adventist settlement, "Advent Town," located west of the town in the Dry Creek Valley.

One

FIRST PEOPLE

Southern Pomo and Western Wappo peoples have been linked to this land for thousands of years. Before photographs or written records, the Russian River (*Ashokawna* in Southern Pomo), its tributary, Dry Creek (*Mihilakawna*), and a generous landscape provided the first peoples and their descendants with a varied and abundant diet. When Europeans first appeared in the Russian River valley in the 1820s, the Southern Pomo village *Kale* existed where the Healdsburg Plaza is today, in the shadow of *Tsuno* (Fitch Mountain). Disruption of Native American culture and settlement patterns began with the establishment of Spanish/Mexican missions in Northern California in the early 1800s and was intensified by the waves of gold seekers and settlers in the 1850s.

After thousands of years of stability, the Southern Pomo and Western Wappo population in the Healdsburg vicinity declined drastically, dropping from an estimated 8,500 people in the 1840s to barely 100 people by 1916, due to newly introduced diseases. The loss of hunting and gathering territory, forced labor, relocation to Mendocino County reservations, and other hardships also took a heavy toll. Most survived by working as migrant agricultural laborers on local ranches. Descendants of these first peoples continue to live and work in the local area. To this day, the Southern Pomo and Western Wappo peoples retain strong personal ties to their homeland and cultural heritage.

This serene image of the river and the mountain evokes a previous time, before roads and bridges were built and new names were given to the old names.

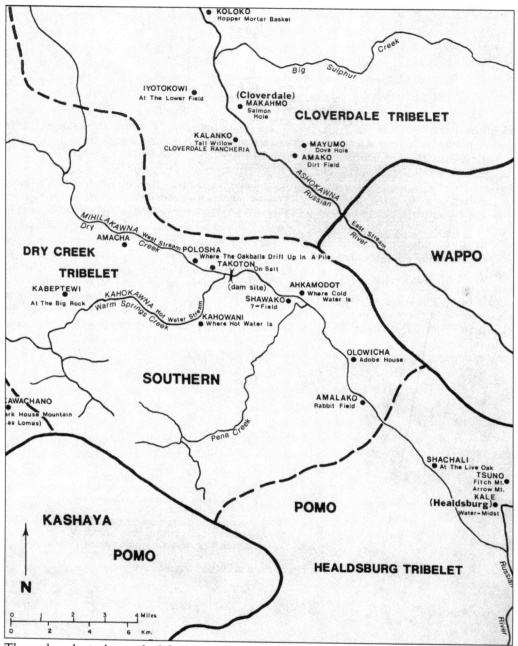

The archaeological record of the Healdsburg area indicates that Native Americans have lived in this region for at least 12,000 years. In the more recent past, Southern Pomo speakers have resided in the vicinity of Healdsburg and Dry Creek Valley. Western Wappo–speaking peoples, who were culturally very similar to the Southern Pomo, lived in Alexander Valley and Geyserville. For generations, they lived in settled, independent villages within recognized home territories. (Map by Terry A. Jackson, 1984.)

This unidentified Southern Pomo man, photographed in front of a fishing weir at the Russian River near Healdsburg, holds two willow fish traps that he probably made himself. Weirs (fences of woven stakes and shoots) were erected seasonally to help block passage of steelhead and salmon. Fish traps would then be placed in front of the weirs. The double-mouth design of the trap allowed fish to enter, but prevented their escape. (Courtesy of the University of Pennsylvania Museum of Archaeology and Anthropology.)

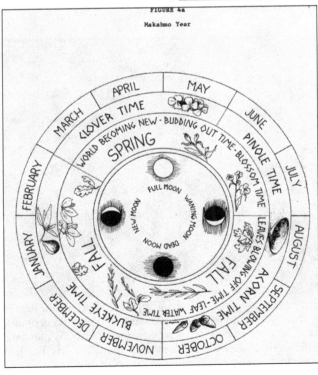

FIGURE 4a

Makahmo Year

Life for the successful hunter-gatherers was closely tied to the seasons. As food resources became available throughout the year, indigenous women gathered and processed berries, seeds, nuts, roots, greens, mushrooms, and tubers. Large quantities of food were collected and stored, to be eaten during the winter months. Men fished and hunted deer, elk, rabbit, other mammals, and birds. (Illustration by Rusty Rossman, 1984.)

Artfully combining form and function, the Southern Pomo and Western Wappo are credited with weaving some of the most complex and beautiful baskets in the world. Laura Fish Somersal, a renowned basket maker of Geyserville Wappo–Dry Creek Pomo ancestry, became a consultant late in life, helping to share and preserve the language and cultural traditions of her people. (Courtesy of the estate of Scott M. Patterson.)

Unlike most basketmaking peoples, Southern Pomo and Western Wappo used both major basket-weaving techniques—coiling and twining. Men and women wove baskets, although generally men wove the simpler "work" baskets. The women were the acknowledged artists. Willow and redbud shoots, and sedge, pine, and bulrush roots were used to create the many designs. Feathers and beads were sometimes added for extra adornment. (Courtesy of Daniel F. Murley.)

Local weavers made a variety of utilitarian baskets to use in harvesting, catching, carrying, cooking, and storing staple foods, such as acorns, salmon, and seeds. Native women fashioned cradle baskets to carry their infants, and exquisite gift baskets to commemorate special events. Pictured here about 1905 are Emma Jeff Manuel and son Frank. A cradle basket enabled a mother to have her hands free while carrying her baby snugly and securely on her back.

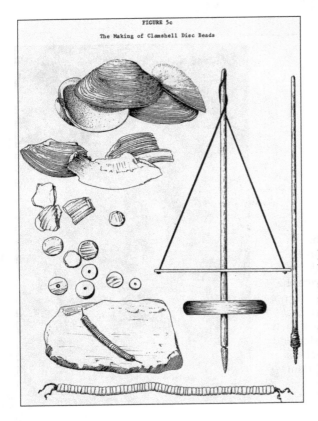

FIGURE 5c

The Making of Clamshell Disc Beads

For both Southern Pomo and Western Wappo, beads were a sign of wealth and status. They were worn as jewelry and used as currency. Pomo men were accomplished bead makers. To make clamshell disc beads, they drilled holes in pieces of shell using a pump drill with a metal tip, like the one pictured here. Earlier they used a handheld drill with a stone tip. (Illustration by Rusty Rossman, 1984.)

Maria Copa Freas, left, is pictured in 1927 at the Alexander Valley Rancheria. When the U.S. government established the Alexander Valley Rancheria in 1909 and the Dry Creek Rancheria in the Alexander Valley in 1915, the small land allotments did little to change the marginal conditions of native life. Most local Pomo and Wappo continued to subsist as migrant laborers.

Elizabeth Dollar and her children, Ruth, Gilbert, and Lena, were photographed in 1925 at the Dry Creek Rancheria in Alexander Valley. Dry Creek and Stewarts Point were the only rancherias in Sonoma County that did not vote for termination when the Rancheria Act was passed in 1958. Other local bands lost their recognized tribal status when they voted to end ties to the government and transfer rancheria land to private ownership. (C. Hart Merriam photograph; courtesy of Bancroft Library, University of California, Berkeley).

In the early 1900s, most native people in the area worked and lived on ranches in exchange for wages and crops, supplementing their diets with whatever traditional foods they could still hunt and gather. This unidentified local family, photographed in front of their dwelling around 1910 by Mervyn Silberstein, worked on the Grant and Minaglia ranches on what is today Bailhache Avenue.

Music and dance were, and still are, integral to Pomo and Wappo cultural life. Seasonal ceremonies, featuring feasting, singing, and dancing, are traditionally celebrated to maintain spiritual balance, give thanks, and renew the world. Dancers wear elaborate regalia, such as the men pictured here in flicker feather headdresses, c. 1928. Their dance imitated precisely the movements of birds. Pictured here, from left to right, are (first row) Henry Arnold, Manuel Cordova, Mike Cordova, and Alfred Elgin; (second row) Elizabeth Dollar, Maggie Waho, Jack Waho, Emma Lozinto, Ruth Cordova, and Lizzie Waho. Mary Lucas is at right in the background.

In the 1930s and 1940s, many native people attended local schools and colleges, and entered nonagricultural careers. In 1942, the Smiths, a prominent Dry Creek Pomo family, hired S. E. Langhart to take this portrait. Bill Smith established the Native American Studies departments at Sonoma State University and Santa Rosa Junior College. His siblings also distinguished themselves in their respective fields. Smith descendants still live in the Healdsburg area. Pictured here, from left to right, are (first row) Douglas and Kathleen Smith; (second row) Marceline (Marcy), Lucy Lozinto, Steve Smith, and Stanley Smith; (third row) Russell, Geraldine (June), and William (Bill) Smith.

Two

BRAVE OLD DAYS

Healdsburg was the idea of a young pioneer merchant, Harmon Heald, who in the early 1850s set up a store on the site of the present town to serve miners taking the main trail to the northern Sierra gold diggings. Another American, Cyrus Alexander, was there before him in the 1840s as ranch manager for Capt. Henry Delano Fitch of San Diego. Fitch, a Yankee sea trader, became a Mexican citizen and acquired the vast Rancho Sotoyome. After the American takeover of California, Fitch's widow, Josefa Carrillo Fitch, moved to the rancho with her large family. She was obliged to sell off portions to pay family debts in 1856 and one of the buyers was Heald. In 1857, he laid out the new town around a plaza.

Alexander was a success as Fitch's agent and was rewarded with the fertile valley north of town that bears his name. He became one of the affluent citizens of Healdsburg in its early years, as did Roderick N. Matheson, a prominent landowner and civic benefactor. Matheson was visiting Washington, D.C., when the Civil War broke out in 1861. He joined the Union army as an infantry colonel and died in battle at age 38. His remains were given a hero's burial in Healdsburg's Oak Mound Cemetery.

Cyrus Alexander's early enterprise as a pioneer rancher in the Alexander Valley made him a rich man. This impressive home, depicted in the 1877 Sonoma County Atlas, was built for his wife, Rufena Lucero, whom he married in 1844. They moved to the home in 1845 and subsequently had 12 children. In 1877, the home was occupied by the widowed Mrs. Alexander, her husband having died in 1872.

In 1825, Henry Delano Fitch, a Yankee sea captain trading along the west coast of South American and Mexico, put into the Mexican port of San Diego. He converted to Roman Catholicism and prevailed over local authorities to marry the beautiful, young Josefa Carrillo. In 1833, Fitch became a Mexican citizen. He acquired from Mexican officials some 48,800 acres of land in Northern California.

Josefa Carrillo fell in love with Capt. Henry Fitch in San Diego and eloped with him to Valparaiso, Chile, where they were married in 1829 when she was 18. They returned to San Diego in 1830 with a son. The Mexican authorities allowed them to "legally" marry and the couple had 10 more children. Fitch died in 1849, never having seen the land he had acquired in Northern California. His widow and nine of their children moved to the Rancho Sotoyome in what is now the Healdsburg region. She died in 1893.

The original home on this site south of the Russian River was built of adobe blocks in 1844 by pioneer Cyrus Alexander for the owner of the land, sea captain Henry Fitch of San Diego. The house was occupied by his widow, Josefa Carrillo Fitch, and their children. In 1878, "Fitch's Castle" was remodeled to contain 17 rooms. It burned down in 1913. The two palm trees remain today.

Anita Fitch Grant, shown here at the height of fashion, *c.* 1883, was born in 1848 in San Diego to Capt. Henry Delano Fitch and Josefa Carrillo de Fitch. She and her siblings were taken by the widowed Mrs. Fitch in 1850 to the vast family rancho in what is now the Healdsburg region. She married John Delano Grant, a former gold seeker and prominent citizen. She died at age 84 in 1933, survived by four children. Courtesy of Sonoma County Library.)

Cyrus Alexander was the first American settler in what became the Healdsburg region. He arrived in 1840 to scout out territory obtained by Capt. Henry Fitch from the Mexican authorities. Fitch then hired Alexander to develop Rancho Sotoyome. In return for his success in this venture, Alexander claimed the wine-growing valley that bears his name. In 1872, he died at his valley ranch.

Pioneer settler Cyrus Alexander built an adobe home in what became the Alexander Valley. The main building was severely damaged in the earthquake of 1906 and demolished. An adobe structure survived and has since been restored and enlarged. This contemporary photograph shows the adobe outbuilding prior to restoration by owners Harry and Maggie Wetzel.

The depiction of Duval D. Phillips's home and abundant farm land in the Dry Creek Valley appeared in the *Sonoma County Atlas*, 1877. Eleven years earlier, he and a partner bought 132 acres from Jose German Piña, who owned the Tzabaco Rancho, a 17,000-acre Mexican land grant. The sale included Piña's adobe house, which later was incorporated into the new two-story house.

Josefa Carrillo Fitch was the widow of Capt. Henry Fitch, who obtained a large land grant in Northern California during the Mexican era. After the American takeover, she was forced to sell property on the Sotoyome Rancho to pay off family debts in 1856. The legal owners brought suit to evict squatters on the land, and eventually force was brought to bear in the short-lived "Squatters' War."

Guardian's Sale.

STATE OF CALIFORNIA, } ss.
In Probate Court, Sonoma County.

BY VIRTUE OF AN ORDER AND DEcree of this Court, made on the 5th day of February. A. D. 1856, I. Josefa Carrillo de Fitch, guardian of Joseph Fitch. Josaphine Fitch, John Fitch, Isabel Fitch, Charles Fitch and Anna Fitch, shall proceed to sell all the right, title and interest of said Joseph Fitch. Josaphine Fitch, John Fitch, Isabel Fitch, Charles Fitch and Anna Fitch, in and to the remaining and unsold portion of the Rancho and Lands called Sotoyome, containing about nine square leagues of land, situated in the counties of Sonoma and Mendocino, in said state of California. The said sale will take place at the Court House door, in the town of Santa Rosa, on **Monday the 25th day of August,** A. D., 1856, commencing at 11 o'clock in the forenoon of that day. The said Rancho and Lands will be subdivided into small tracts of convenient size for farming purposes, and sold in separate subdivisions. The terms of sale will be, one third cash, and the balance on a credit not exceeding three years, secured by bond and mortgage on the land, at an interest of one per cent. per month, payable semi-annually.

JOSEFA CARRILLO DE FITCH,
51-3w   Guardian, &c.

Healdsburg's founder, Harmon Heald, left Missouri to come to the California gold fields but ended up in Sonoma County. He chose a location on the main road, built a small cabin, and soon added a small store. The site he chose was to become the town of Healdsburg, and his cabin was located on West Street (now Healdsburg Avenue). Heald laid out the town and donated land for the Plaza and lots for a school, cemetery, and churches. Heald did not live to see his town develop; he died of consumption in 1858 at the age of 34 years.

Sarah Heald Shaw, the sister of Healdsburg's founder Harmon Heald, was a single young woman when she joined her brothers in California in 1851. She married T. A. Shaw in 1852 and lived in the Healdsburg settlement where her son, Thomas, the first of three children, was born in 1853. Widowed in the 1860s, she raised her family in Cloverdale.

In 1861, Roderick N. Matheson, a prominent landowner and civic benefactor of Healdsburg, traveled to Washington, D.C., seeking a political appointment. Instead, the Civil War started and he enlisted in the Union Army. Infantry colonel Matheson was killed in battle the following year at age 38. His remains were buried with great ceremony in Healdsburg's Oak Mound Cemetery.

In 1844, Antoinette "Netty" Seaman married Roderick N. Matheson in New York City. She is pictured here with her infant son Roderick Jr., who was born in 1849. His father hoped that Roddy would attend West Point, but that wasn't to be. Roderick Jr., died in a threshing machine accident in the Sacramento Valley. After Colonel Matheson was killed in the Battle of Crampton's Gap in 1862, Netty lived in the Matheson home in Healdsburg until her death in 1884.

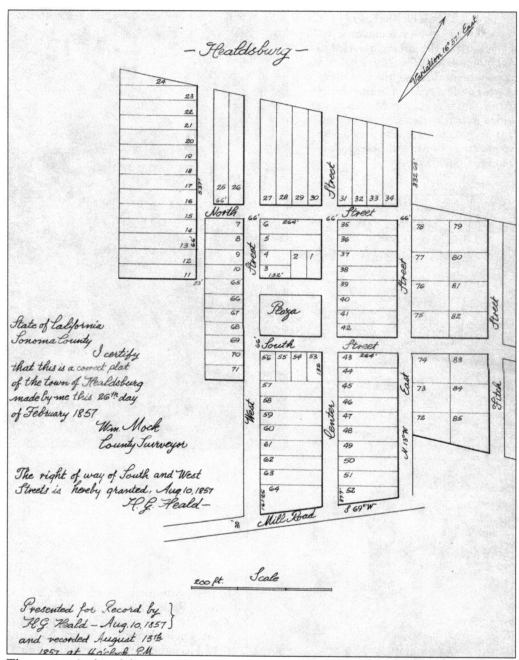

The surveyor's plat of the town Harmon Heald laid out around a central plaza was recorded by Sonoma County authorities in August 1857. The new owners of the Healdsburg lots began paying county taxes that year, according to 1857–1858 tax records. Early in the development, lots were said to be selling for $15, but real estate prices quickly escalated.

Three

BUILDERS OF OUR HERITAGE

In the early years, there were a few residences on the Plaza's boundary streets, but retail stores and professional services were predominant, including the office of colorful attorney Lewis A. Norton. He was elected president of the board of trustees in 1867, when the town incorporated. The most substantial building in the 19th century was Healdsburg's city hall, a handsome three-story brick edifice built diagonally across from the southeast corner of the Plaza in 1886, when the town had great municipal ambitions. Diagonally across the Plaza, the Union Hotel was a solid brick anchor on West Street (now Healdsburg Avenue). Beside it was the Rosenberg and Bush department store, founded in 1865 and operated by three-generations of the civic-minded Rosenberg family. The Young funeral service was another three-generation business.

The 20th century brought a wave of improvements. The first water main reached the center of town in 1900 through a system that boasted 42 fire hydrants. The energetic Ladies Improvement Club celebrated by donating a four-sided public drinking fountain. The automotive age arrived, but a hitching rail around the Plaza still accommodated farmer's wagons in the early decades. The Farmers and Mechanics Bank, founded in 1877, opened a new building on the northeast corner of the Plaza in 1908. The building still stands today.

In 1859, trees grow in the main thoroughfare of the new town. A contemporary source observed, "The road through Healdsburg shows a fine disregard for traffic hazards such as trees in the street." This is a view looking south on West Street (now Healdsburg Avenue). The Union Hotel with a second-floor veranda is on the right, and the Plaza is out of view on the left.

MADRONA TREE, HEALDSBURG, CALIFORNIA.

This madrone tree at the intersection of Powell Street (now Plaza Street) and West Street (now Healdsburg Avenue) on the northwest corner of the Plaza caught the eye of an English travel writer in the 1860s and was reproduced as a line engraving in his book on California experiences. At that time, the Plaza was lightly forested with original growth, including madrone and oak.

A rare snow fall of about 10 inches on Wednesday, December 3, 1873, brought this young couple to Center Street on the Plaza in a horse-drawn sleigh that looks to have been improvised from a buckboard seat. The *Russian River Flag* said, "The boys of the town were out in force and freely indulged in the pastime of snow-balling each other as well as passers-by."

Horse teams and drivers dig a trench for the first water main down West Street (now Healdsburg Avenue) across from the Plaza in January 1900. Water from a newly constructed reservoir served more than eight miles of pipe and 42 fire hydrants. A sign marks the location of Gray and Byington hardware and plumbing, a new business to meet the needs of city water customers. It had been a grocery store a few months before.

This c. 1907 image looks out from the upper story of the old city hall northwest across the Plaza. Horse-drawn vehicles dominate the scene, but a closer look discloses two automobiles parked at curbs on the north and west—a hint of things to come. The classic facade of the Farmers and Mechanics Bank on the right remains across from the Plaza's northeast corner.

This 1867 view east toward what is now the intersection of Matheson and Center Streets shows the Plaza being used as a handy parking area for farm wagons in the early years of the town. The office of attorney Lewis A. Norton is marked by a sign on a corner of the intersection. In 1867, Norton was elected president of the first city board of trustees, which met in this office.

Freight cars waiting to be loaded, or unloaded, are at the first Healdsburg Depot about 1890. The Oak Lawn Hotel, located behind the trees, catered to railroad passengers. Fitch Mountain provides the backdrop for this local scene.

In the summer of 1871, Joseph Downing opened his "Photograph Rooms" on Center Street on the east side of the Plaza. His father was a Healdsburg furniture maker and undertaker who brought his family from Massachusetts via the Isthmus of Panama in 1857. Joseph Downing returned to the East in 1869 to study photography. He left town in 1879 to pursue his career, but settled again in Healdsburg late in life.

This c. 1921 advertising postcard for Healdsburg's Rosenberg and Bush department store evokes nostalgia for a simpler time with a floral-framed image of puppies and a boy in a sailor suit. The store, founded in 1865 by Wolfe Rosenberg, was the leading family-owned, dry-goods retailer in town for three generations. (Courtesy of Christine Coon.)

The Cook and Garrett Hardware store, c. 1890, was located on the 300 block of Center Street next to the Gobbi Building. The firm advertised "plumbing and tinning" and sold Cyclone windmills and Universal stoves. In 1892, the business moved into the Gobbi location. Garrett Hardware and Plumbing Company continues to do business in Healdsburg.

The patriotic bunting on the street sweeper's cart indicates a special occasion on the Plaza in the late 1890s. The view is east on Matheson Street toward a "Welcome" banner at the intersection of Center Street. Beyond is the extensive Matheson property where in July 1897, a cavalry troop of the National Guard, San Francisco, made camp after riding through town. The occasion would have called out the street sweeper.

The Young funeral establishment became a three-generation business in Healdsburg. This mid-1890s photograph shows founder John Young (right) standing on the sidewalk with his son Thomas (center). Another son, Eben "Ted" Young, is seated on the hearse next to driver, Harry Cummings. Thomas' son Fred took over the business in 1919 after his father's death, changing the name to Fred Young and Company.

In 1909, proprietors and customers of the Dry Creek Store, located in the heart of Dry Creek Valley farmland, line up in the shaded wagon way for a picture. The owners, Mr. Boyce (left) and Mrs. Boyce (in the doorway), sold the business in 1917 to Lloyd and Lydia Goodyear, who operated it for many years. The store, established in 1881, remains in business today at the same location on Dry Creek Road.

Town folk in their holiday finery assemble in the Plaza, c. 1906. The muddy street surface in the foreground was improved with pavement in the next decade. City hall, the brick structure commanding the southeast corner of the square on the right, was dedicated in 1886. It was torn down in the 1960s to make way for a more modest building. The traditional spire in the center of the photograph marks St. John's Catholic Church, now replaced with a modern church.

In 1901, a grand drinking fountain in the center of the Plaza was donated to the city by the Ladies Improvement Club. The ladies were given permission to tear down a popular bandstand to make way for the fountain. This caused controversy and petitions were circulated, but the club prevailed. Healdsburg's first city hall anchors this c. 1910 view to the southeast corner. Twenty-five years after its installation, the fountain was replaced by a flagpole. The benches pictured in the center are still in place today.

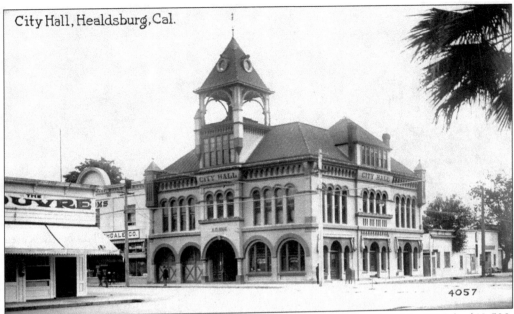

City Hall, Healdsburg, Cal.

4057

Healdsburg's first city hall was this three-story brick masterwork completed in 1886 for $12,500. It housed city offices and also provided space in the early years for the library, firemen's quarters, courts, and jail. After 74 years of service, it was deemed an "eyesore" by the *Healdsburg Tribune* and demolished in 1960. The location at the southeast corner of Center and Matheson Streets is now commercial property.

THE LOUVRE

The Louvre restaurant—not to be confused with the Louvre Museum in Paris—operated at the northeast corner of Matheson and Center Streets, across from the City Hall, into the early decades of the 20th century. The group in front includes the businessmen and farmers who dined at the Louvre. The restaurant advertised "Quick and First Class Service" and "Plain Meals 25 cents."

In the early years of the 20th century, as automotive traffic increased in the Plaza business area, there was an attempt to accommodate farmers and others who still relied on the horse. Wagons and carriages could be tied to the hitching rail around the Plaza. The view looking north on West Street (now Healdsburg Avenue) shows parked cars using the surrounding curbs.

The Healdsburg salesroom of Studebaker dealer N. A. Seipel illustrates a transitional period in the transportation industry in the second decade of the 20th century. Motor cars share space with wagons and carriages on the main floor. The gallery is devoted to horse-powered vehicles. In the foreground is a child's wagon.

In 1908, the Farmers and Mechanics Bank, located at the northwest corner of Powell (now Plaza) and Center Streets, was under construction. George Day, standing fourth from left, was contractor for the building. This was the second bank building in Healdsburg—and the first bank in the county to use a time lock on its safe. *The Russian River Flag* noted that the "counting room is commodious." This handsome building is still standing today.

An arch of milk bottles hangs over the entrance to H. C. LeBaron's creamery, established in 1932 in the old Farmers and Mechanics Bank building on the Plaza at Powell (now Plaza) and Center Streets. The plant bottled milk and cream and produced ice cream, butter, and cheese. The creamery offered soda fountain service on site and, as the odd mix of advertising makes clear, sold both draft and bottled beer.

In 1911, the Carnegie Library is shown here near completion of construction. It was made possible by a $10,000 grant from industrialist Andrew Carnegie. The town provided the site on Matheson Street at Fitch Street. The library, previously housed in quarters at city hall, expanded into this neoclassical revival building designed by prominent Petaluma architect Brainerd Jones.

In 1988, the Healdsburg Library was added to the National Register of Historic Places. In 1990, the building was renovated to become the home of the Healdsburg Museum and Historical Society.

Four

INTENT ON LEARNING

Education was important to the early settlers. The Russian River Institute, a private school, was organized and built in 1857, the same year Healdsburg was founded. University Street was named in its honor. The first public elementary school was built in 1871 on Tucker Street. The school soon expanded and, by 1880, had 227 students. Public high school instruction was first offered in 1888, and in 1891, the school graduated nine scholars (eight girls and one boy) before a crowd of 600 proud townspeople.

The Seventh-day Adventist Church operated the Healdsburg College at Fitch and Powell Streets (now Plaza Court) from 1882 to about 1906, offering a variety of academic and vocational courses. In 1906, the public school trustees built a two-story, 11-room grammar school on the original Tucker Street site. The main stone building was torn down in 1934 because of concerns over earthquake safety. A mission-style school replaced it at North and First Streets. In 1954, a new high school building was constructed at Powell Avenue and Prince Street.

The Healdsburg Albanian Literary and Military Society was formed by a group of 25 young ladies who met weekly in the 1880s to discuss authors and musicians. In addition, to the delight of Healdsburg citizens, they performed marching drills in their red, white, and blue uniforms. Members pictured here, from left to right, are (first row) Minnie Reynolds McMullin, Emma Truitt Petray, May Shaw, and Artie Griest; (second row) Emma Logan Beeson, Millie Emerson Phillips, and Sara Sullivan Ross. The little drummer girl is not identified.

The Russian River Institute was built in 1857, the year Healdsburg was founded, on a site that became University Street between Tucker and Haydon Streets. It was the town's first private school. This *c.* 1875 photograph shows faculty and students in the school's open windows on the second floor, while uncomfortable boys in formal attire are in front of the trim picket fence.

In 1879, the student body and faculty members gather for a formal portrait in front of the Healdsburg Institute. Illustrating the town's early emphasis on higher education, the building was constructed in 1877 in the area around Plaza Court off Fitch Street. Prof. Heber Thomson was principal. The institute merged with the Alexander Academy in 1880 to become the Healdsburg Academy.

The third-grade class at Healdsburg College, c. 1890, shows off their handmade brooms created as part of a practical curriculum that offered more than academic studies. Boys and girls were instructed in shoemaking, tent making, blacksmithing, tailoring, and dressmaking. Boys also helped care for farm animals and girls had domestic duties. The Seventh-day Adventist Church, which ran the college, left Healdsburg in 1908 and reopened in Napa County as Pacific Union College.

In 1882, the Healdsburg College was founded by the Seventh-day Adventists at Fitch and Powell (now Plaza) Streets and had annual enrollments as high as 200 students during its more than 20 years of operation. The institution, renamed the Pacific Union College, relocated to Angwin in Napa County, where it remains today.

Students of Grant School on Old Redwood Highway assemble for a *c.* 1915 picture with their teacher, right. The 39 children of various ages on display here demonstrate the demands on lone teachers of grades one through eight. The school was named for the family of John Delano Grant, a prominent rancher. The building later converted to a private residence. (Courtesy of Louis J. Foppiano.)

This group of students, with their teacher at the wheel, poses in front of the Geyserville Grammar School in 1914. Before 1915, Geyserville teenagers had to commute to Healdsburg to attend high school. By 1936, the one-room grammar schools of the Lincoln, Hamilton, Canyon, Oriental, and Independence School Districts were consolidated into the Geyserville School District. In 1943, Peña School was added. (Courtesy of the Sonoma County Library.)

The keystone is set in the entrance arch of the Healdsburg Grammar School during construction in 1906. The building crew, many of them skilled stone workers who emigrated from Italy, gathers around for the event. In 1934, this main building of the grammar school was declared an earthquake hazard and torn down.

The 11-room Healdsburg Grammar School, completed in 1906, was financed by a bond issue of $35,000, approved by the voters in May 1905. It replaced an elementary school built in 1871.

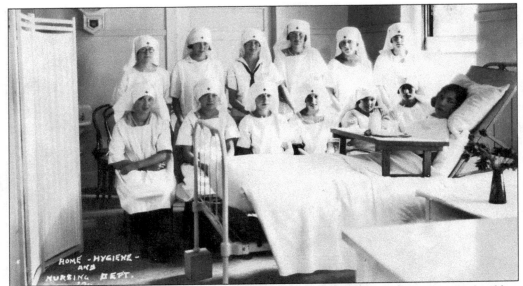

The home room of the hygiene and nursing department of the Healdsburg Grammar School has been transformed into a demonstration hospital facility in this 1924 photograph. Girls were urged to consider nursing as a career—12 of them are seen here wearing professional-looking caps and uniforms. A meal has been served the "patient."

On a February day in 1936, the student body of Mill Creek School assembled for the photographer. The teacher, Mrs. Clara Schieffer on the left, taught grades one through eight as was the custom of small rural schools of the time. The community of Mill Creek, west of Healdsburg, grew up around the first mill established in the region in the early 1850s.

Isabella Agnes Farlinger

7-26-18

Healdsburg High School
Faculty 7-26-18

In July 1918, the faculty of Healdsburg High School forms up at the entrance of the new school building during ceremonies celebrating its construction. Among them were teachers whose subjects included Latin and ancient history, Spanish and music, and science and athletics. The *Healdsburg Tribune* proudly reported every classroom had a telephone connection to the principal's office. The enrollment was 172.

Four new buses of the Healdsburg High School were lined up to be admired on the east side of the Plaza at the start of the fall term, September 1922. "They are finished in battleship gray with black trimmings and have the letters 'H. H .S.' in gold on both sides," the *Healdsburg Tribune* reported. The buses had upholstered seats for 30 passengers. It was "palatial" service for students from rural districts, the paper said.

Salvation Army Capt. Wilfred C. Bourne, left, was the first superintendent of the Lytton Springs Orphanage from 1904 to 1916. In the early years, the orphanage accepted very young children. The age for admission was later changed to between six and 15 years. Here a little new arrival is matched up with a garment by one of the women on staff.

The gentleman in the middle is San Francisco's Mayor James "Sunny Jim" Rolph, wearing his trademark boutonniere. The occasion is the dispatch of what appears to be a gift flower box to the wife of Pres. Calvin Coolidge, c. 1926. On the right is Lt. Col. Wilfred C. Bourne of the Salvation Army's Lytton Orphanage, north of Healdsburg.

This booklet, published by the Salvation Army in December 1937, said there were 220 boys and girls living in the Lytton home at the time. The broken homes of the Depression added to the population. "They are victims of unhappy circumstances over which they had no control." The superintendent, Major R. H. Simpson, and his wife had a staff of 33 to care for their charges.

It was the practice of Healdsburg newspapers in the early years of the 20th century to log the admission of children to the Lytton home. The *Healdsburg Enterprise* printed this account in January 20, 1912. A half orphan was a child with one surviving parent. During its 54 years of service, the home for boys and girls cared for some 11,000 children.

ORPHAN CHILDREN

The following orphans and half-orphans have been received at the Golden Gate Orphanage at Lytton from Oct. 1st., to Jan. 6th., 1912.

HALF ORPHANS

Clarence Hanson	9 years
Anna Hanson	6 years
Pete Corel'l	4 years
Russel Badger	8 eyars
Dora Barboez	2 years
Amelia Barboez	8 mos.
Berna Baker	4 years
Alfred Baker	6 years
John Spellacy	10 years
Arthur Spellacy	8 years
Earl Russell	10 years
Ray Smith	6 years

ORPHANS

Chester Boyce	9 years
John Hanoran	9 years

C. W. BOURNE, Major.

The children of the Salvation Army Boys and Girls Home and Farm helped out with chores as part of a training program to equip them for work in the outside world. Here girls scatter feed to some of the 2000 White Leghorn and New Hampshire chickens on the farm in the 1930s. Fresh eggs from the chickens were an important part of the diet at the home.

SOME OF THE LYTTON GRADUATES LATER TOOK AGRICULTURE AS THEIR LIFE'S WORK.

Boys are at play aboard this tractor, but agricultural training was a serious pursuit as the Lytton Springs Orphanage evolved into the Salvation Army Boys and Girls Home and Farm in the early decades of the 20th century. By the 1930s, the home operated a farm of 800 acres, including orchards, vegetable gardens, and prize-winning livestock. Boys on barn duty got up at 5:00 a.m.

This new administration building for the Salvation Army Boys and Girls Home and Farm at Lytton Springs, north of Healdsburg, was dedicated in January 1921. In 1920, the old resort hotel that the Salvation Army took over when it founded the orphanage in 1904, burned down. The new building held offices, a dining room, a kitchen, and a dormitory for girls. The boys, some of whom are shown here, lived in cottages on the grounds.

A vintage car and a contingent of boys with farming tools on their shoulders start out from the grounds of the Salvation Army's Lytton Springs home for a Future Farmers Parade in Healdsburg, c. 1950. Teenagers from the home attended Healdsburg High School and the town made sure the youngsters were part of community events. The facility closed in 1958 after 54 years of operation.

Five

JOYFUL PURSUITS

In 1847, an American bear hunter discovered a wild canyon in Northern California where steam spewed from vents in the earth and the air reeked with the smell of sulphur. This amazing place became known as The Geysers, although technically the steam was produced from fumaroles. In Victorian society, The Geysers were more than a natural wonder. They allowed visitors to pursue an alleged therapeutic regime of mineral water and hot spring baths. Healdsburg was a staging point for visitors prepared to take the five-hour journey north over perilous roads.

The Russian River offered abundant fish for the angler and it was a boater's idyllic dream early in the 20th century. Others embraced the automobile and aviation ages. In the middle of the century, the river between the bridges became the arena where more enthusiastic water sports were pursued, including a novelty—women's wine barrel racing. The community vigorously promoted the summer resorts developed on the river beside Fitch Mountain. Locals played closer to home at Merryland Beach, now Memorial Beach, and dined at the Ark Restaurant on the river's bank.

In 1926, Madeline Moore, Faith Powell, and Paloma Grant appear to be cooking lunch on a steam vent in this publicity shot at The Geysers.

Tourists hike carefully through The Geysers canyon, getting close to the spewing fumaroles. The loud noise of escaping steam and the pungent sulphur odor did not deter visitors to one of California's most popular natural wonders in the late 19th century. Bear hunter Bill Elliott discovered the canyon in 1847.

One of the appeals of The Geysers to 19th century visitors staying at The Geysers Hotel was the supposed therapeutic value of drinking mineral water from hot springs and soaking in warm water baths. American enterprise saw the commercial advantage of bottling the mineral water at the source and bringing it to consumers around the country. The copy for this *c.* 1880 bottled water advertisement has a familiar ring.

In 1881, a stage loaded down with luggage and freight on the rear platform and roof takes the Calistoga and Lakeport Road up Mount St. Helena to neighboring Lake County. The driver is Joe Johns. It is summer and the California panorama of tawny hills rolls out before the road.

Stages pulled by six-horse teams conveyed tourists, many of them distinguished visitors from the East, to The Geysers over a rough road with steep falloffs on either side. Driver Clark Foss's daredevil style at the reins made him a local legend. A September 1869 edition of the *Russian River Flag* described a hair-raising trip with Foss, concluding that his eight-year, accident-free record assured riders of "comparative safety."

Renowned stagecoach driver Clark Foss originated and drove the passenger lines along a mountainous route from Healdsburg to The Geysers, and later from Calistoga to the world-famous hot springs during the 1850s and 1860s. The six-foot, two-inch, 220-pound Foss was considered by a contemporary writer "not only an unequaled driver, but a man of genius and a philosopher."

In 1875, Bostwick and Emerson, proprietors of the Geyser Livery and Stage Stable, ran daily stages to the Geyser Springs, a popular Victorian resort. The route went northeast through the quicksilver mining area of Pine Flat and Mercuryville and along the vertiginous Hogsback Ridge. The stages left at 6:00 a.m. and returned at 6:00 p.m. The firm also rented saddle horses and turnouts (horse-drawn carriages).

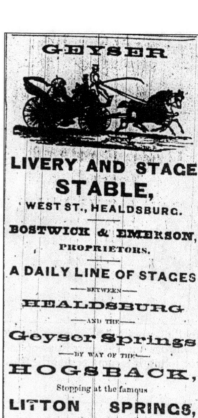

The Geysers, one of the most popular natural wonders of California in the 19th century, elevated Healdsburg from the status of remote farm town to important staging point for out-of-state visitors. Here, c. 1860s–1870s, the typical California stage, with canvas sides rolled up, gets ready to roll. Calistoga in Napa County to the east offered a competing service. Stages continued to make the run into the 20th century. (Courtesy of the Society of California Pioneers, San Francisco.)

By 1916, Ray Lattin's Auto Stage transported both guests and the U. S. mail to and from The Geysers. Foss's horses no longer made the hair-raising trip up the hills. Lattin's Stanley Steamer gave a more sedate ride, even though he had to stop and back up to make it around some of the turns and it was common to stop and draw water for the engine from a creek.

A party of horseback riders mounts up on the site of the abandoned mining community of Mercuryville, *c.* the 1920s. Founded in 1874, Mercuryville was one of a number of hasty settlements that flourished and faded in the quicksilver mining district northwest of Healdsburg. The building here served as a gasoline station and refreshment stand on the road to The Geysers.

This foot bridge across The Geysers canyon led to three caves carved into the hillside. These sweat caves were used by the indigenous people long before the tourist rush of the 19th century. The natural steam heated the caves in temperatures from hot, to hotter, to hottest. Visitors sat on benches, sweated away their troubles, and re-crossed the bridge to cool in a mineral water pool.

The Geysers Hotel, built about 1868, replaced the canvas tents and cabins that accommodated early visitors. Hunting in the rough terrain surrounding the resort was a popular pursuit. Here a hunting party relaxes in the shade of the oak tree. Their kill, which appears to be a boar, hangs from the tree. (Courtesy of the Society of California Pioneers, San Francisco.)

In 1915, holiday bunting drapes an open-air dance hall at The Geysers, northeast of Healdsburg. The hall was an apparent attempt to broaden the social attraction of the former fashionable health spa as other, more convenient resorts were developed along the Russian River. In the 1930s, the old hotel at The Geysers burned down.

One of the earliest automobiles in town, the 1902 Locomobile with tiller steering, rolls through the Plaza with W. T. Albertson, a lumber mill owner, and his wife aboard in proper driving attire. There was a 14-inch boiler beneath the seat which provided the steam for the twin-cylinder engine. Much of the running gear consisted of bicycle parts.

These young ladies display the high spirits that made them a popular, ukulele-playing, rooting section for the Healdsburg High School's athletic teams. The ukulele club was formed in 1916, and also performed away from the sports field at recitals featuring "old plantation songs and popular Hawaiian airs."

With airports in short supply, early flyers landed on any convenient pasture. Here a 1918 biplane is the center of attention and was the first airplane to give rides to many locals at the big hop-and-prune ranch of Clarence Hall, located near Healdsburg in the Alexander Valley. The first local airport was the short-lived Athey Field, established in 1941 on a site now occupied by the Healdsburg Hospital.

At the end of World War II, a graded landing strip for airplanes was established on the ranch of brothers Lewis and Edward Norton, fronting the Lytton Springs Road northwest of Healdsburg. Known as the Norton Sky Ranch, it provided popular flight training for returning veterans and students of the Healdsburg High School aviation science class. The dirt strip and hangar facilities were leased to the city in 1962 to become the Healdsburg Municipal Airport.

Formally dressed boaters on the Russian River at Healdsburg create an idyllic scene that appeared on postcards, c. 1910. The boaters are upstream from the rail and road bridges crossing the river on Healdsburg's east side.

These young women—a bevy of beauties in the promotional lexicon of the time—gather for publicity purposes on the beach of the Russian River's Camp Rose, a popular summer resort beside Fitch Mountain. The reason for the eclectic display of bathing costumes in this c. 1920s postcard is lost in time. The black dog waits to plunge into action after the ball.

These young women in fashionable bathing suits hoist a canoe on the bank of the Russian River to demonstrate the recreational possibilities of the Healdsburg area. In this c. 1940 picture are Vivian Micheletti, Alta Badger, Faye Auradou, Eva Rafanelli, Rubye Gambetta, and Adeline Passarino, all residents of Healdsburg.

The summer dam on the Russian River, below the railroad and vehicle bridges, was a recreational tradition established around the turn of the 20th century. The body of water created was called Lake Sotoyome—recalling the name of the original land grant where the town was founded. In this image, two men stroll downstream of the dam toward the spillway while fishermen row on the lake.

One of the final events of the three-day Harvest Festival at the end of August in 1946 was the women's wine barrel race on the Russian River under the highway and railroad bridges behind the summer dam. The participants here, from left to right, are Virginia Patterson, Harriet Carroll, and Barbara Kron. The *Healdsburg Tribune* said the competitors "spent the better part of the week practicing with the tricky drums."

The winner of a wine barrel race in the Russian River, believed to be Lillian Page, gets a victory dunking during the 1946 Harvest Festival with the help of Billie Jo Bennett Haley, one of the finalists. Other participants included Lenora Lewis and Diane Wolking standing to the left behind Haley. Local wine businessman Joe Vercelli, in white shirt sleeves on the right, was one of the race's sponsors. (Courtesy of the Sonoma County Library.)

The Russian River resorts on Fitch Mountain attracted so many tourists during the 1920s, 1930s, and 1940s, that an electric sign was installed at the intersection of West (now Healdsburg Avenue) and Matheson Streets to help direct traffic. Some families from the San Francisco Bay Area returned to the same summer cottage, rental cabin, or campground every year and made lasting friendships and ties to Healdsburg.

When this picture was taken in 1936, the Ark Restaurant, on the west bank of the Russian River below the highway bridge, was a culinary institution in Healdsburg. Proprietors Julio and Gino Sbragia served "delicious Italian food" and fresh fish from the river. The little paddle wheeler could take passengers across to Merryland (now Memorial) Beach.

The elaborate tea service laid out on an exquisite tablecloth waits under a leafy bower for fashionably gowned ladies on the lawn of the Snook residence. The tea party was given in July 1932 by Nettie Cole Snook and her two daughters, Marguerite and Cleone, for Mrs. Snook's niece, Mrs. Ruth Lucas Gilliland of Dallas, Texas.

Six

CHURCHGOING FOLK

The churches that gave the town of Healdsburg its spiritual character began going up the year of its founding in 1857. Among the first was the Methodist Episcopal North Church, located on a lot on the south side of the Plaza. The Methodist Episcopal South Church was built on East Street nearby. Prior to the Civil War, the M. E. church was so divided on the subject of slavery that congregations across the U.S. split into "north" and "south" factions. The Methodists of the "Plaza Church," as it was known, sold their property to the Presbyterians in 1861 and constructed a new church at Fitch and Haydon Streets in 1870. The first elder of the Presbyterian church was pioneer Cyrus Alexander. In 1933, the Methodists and Presbyterians joined to become the Federated Church of Healdsburg. The First Baptist Church, originally given land on the town's south side by Harmon Heald in 1858, built a church in 1868 on a lot on Fitch Street it still occupies. In 1908, the church was remodeled to its present form.

The Seventh-day Adventists established a modest church on North Street in 1871, and later founded a private high school. In 1886, the Adventists constructed one of the town's largest churches at Matheson and Fitch Streets. It was demolished in 1921. Catholics purchased land southeast of Matheson and East Streets in 1873 and in 1910 dedicated a new, two-spired church, St. John the Baptist, which served the growing parish for decades. A guild hall, built for St. Paul's Episcopal Church members in 1888, was moved to a site at Matheson and East Streets in 1900. It was remodeled into a place of worship and has undergone several alterations since. In 1900, the Church of Christ, one of the first organized religions in Healdsburg, built a new church at East and Powell (now Plaza) Streets. It is there today.

Healdsburg photographer S. E. Langhart photographed this group of children in 1924 in their first communion finery in front of the (second) St. John's Catholic Church.

Ellen G. White, founder and prophetess of the Seventh-day Adventist church, penned some of her most influential religious writings while living in Healdsburg in the 1870s. She and her husband, James, moved from West Dry Creek Road to Powell Avenue to be closer to Healdsburg College, the Adventist institution that opened on Fitch Street in 1882. (Courtesy of Elmshaven Historic Site.)

Healdsburg became an important community to the Seventh-day Adventists when Ellen G. White, one of the religion's spiritual leaders in the mid-19th century, took up residence in the town. She was influential in the founding of the Adventists' Healdsburg College in 1882. This image of the Seventh-day Adventist Church, built in 1884 at Fitch and Matheson Streets, is from a college catalog.

Shown here is a 1904 Sunday school class at the Seventh-day Adventist church. The Seventh-day Adventists attracted one of the largest congregations in town at the turn of the century, and built a substantial Gothic Revival church at the corner of Fitch and Matheson streets.

The first Mass was said in Healdsburg in 1860, and the first Catholic church (left) was built in 1873. A new St. John the Baptist Catholic Church (below) was built in 1910 with double spires in a Romanesque style to serve a growing congregation. In 1964, for the same reason, this building gave way to a modern structure on the old location at the southeast corner of Matheson and East Streets.

After singing a full choral service on Easter Sunday 1954, the St. Paul's Episcopal Church choir gathered on the church steps. Standing with the choir is Rev. Frank B. Kent, then St. Paul's minister.

The first Episcopal parish structure was a guild hall, built in 1888 near East and Matheson Streets. In 1900, it was moved to the northeast corner of the intersection. The building was remodeled for worship and St. Paul's Episcopal Church was consecrated in 1913. The church, as seen in this early 1900s picture, has since undergone other architectural changes. The original pews, handmade in 1902, are still in use.

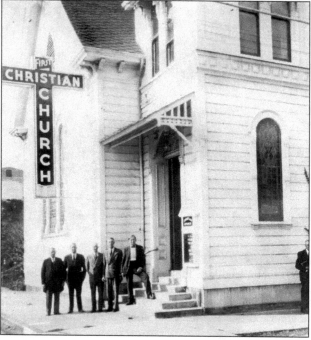

The Christian Church was organized by Elder F. M. Marion in 1857, the same year that Healdsburg was founded. From an original membership of 10, the congregation grew tremendously during the 1880s. In 1892, Santa Rosa contractors Simpson and Roberts built the existing Gothic Revival church. In 1917, some members of the Christian Church joined individuals from the Baptist church to form a new congregation. Since then, the house of worship has been the First Christian Church and is currently known as the Christian Bible Church.

In 1957, this group of young people was confirmed by Rev. Richard Wagner at Good Shepherd Lutheran Church. Pictured here are (first row) Jeanette Jones, Gary Dickson, Martin Johnson, Steve Solem, and Carol Isaacson; (second row) Paul Lewering.

The First Baptist Church was one of the early organized churches in Healdsburg in the 1850s. After meeting at various homes and schools, members built the First Baptist Church on Fitch Street in 1871. In 1908, the original building was moved to the rear of the lot and the present church erected. A distinguishing feature is the central stained glass window depicting "Christ, the Good Shepherd."

The popular chancel choir of the Federated Church sang in Healdsburg, and also performed in churches in the Bay Area. *Ebony* magazine published a 1951 feature about Smith Robinson, the choir director pictured here, leading the group in song. (Courtesy of Marion Hoy Jones.)

In the early 1950s, Smith Robinson, seated second from the right in the front row, took his youth choir of Healdsburg's Federated Church on appearances around the Bay Area. Here they join the Baptist choir of his brother-in-law's church in San Francisco.

Seven

CHAMPIONS AMONG US

The earliest residents of Healdsburg found time for and pursued with passion the goals and standards of athletics and organized team competition. Of particular interest and achievement were the pursuits of track and field and the national pastime of baseball. Many successful and talented local athletes went on to distinguish themselves in the wider world of professional and Olympic sport.

Ralph Rose won a total of six medals at three Olympic games. The six-foot, five-inch, 250 pound Rose was the only man to win national championships in shot put, discus, and javelin, and the first to put the shot more than 50 feet. Track and field Hall of Famer Edward Beeson was world high-jump champion with a record set at 6 feet, 7^1/$_{16}$ inches in 1914. Hazel Hotchkiss Wightman was U.S. National Women's Tennis Singles Champion in 1909, 1910, 1911, and 1919. She also was doubles champion at Wimbledon, and Olympic gold medal doubles winner—both with partner Helen Wills in 1924. On October 24, 1955, Robert A. Boehm, the world's inboard motorboat hydroplane champion, set the record for the 136-cubic-inch engine at 83.89 miles per hour.

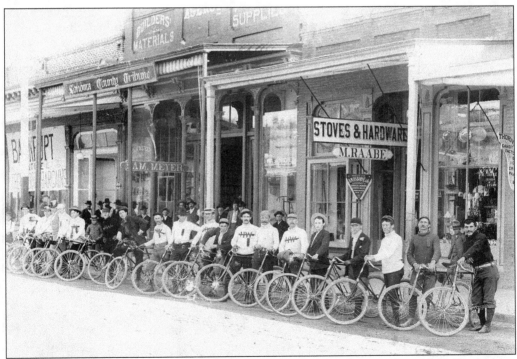

During the bicycle craze at the end of the 19th century, local enthusiasts formed the Healdsburg Wheelmen. The Wheelmen enjoyed riding as a group, showing off their "HW" logo pierced with an arrow. This *c.* 1890 photograph shows them ready to stream off from the Plaza on well-kept bicycles.

In 1871, Dolly Babcock, dressed for a day of equestrian enjoyment, stands beside her mount in downtown Healdsburg. The propriety and comfort of sidesaddle riding was appropriate for women in that day and age.

Healdsburg Athletic Club members gather for a photograph, c. 1895. The club was founded in 1894 with 20 members. Members worked out in the gymnasium in the Gobbi Building on Center Street. The two men reclining in front, one smoking a cigar, probably did not share the dedication to conditioning of the other club members.

The twilight baseball league, which began as an experiment in 1930, had caught on by 1932 when eight local teams—representing businesses, service clubs, and other groups—began playing in May on a diamond next to the American Legion Hall on Center Street between North and Piper Streets. New lights were installed for the 1932 season. The property is now part of a shopping center at that location.

OFFICIAL
Schedule and Score Card
HEALDSBURG
TWILIGHT
BASEBALL LEAGUE

1932 Season

COMPLIMENTS
Healdsburg Tribune

Known affectionately as the "Check Cashers," "The Moneymen," and other even more colorful names, this 1931 Bank of America team played in the highly popular Healdsburg Twilight Baseball League. Manager August Wagele is standing at right.

The Goldstein Brothers, both born in Healdsburg, owned a men's clothing store in town and sponsored a popular and successful baseball team. The 1896 team pictured above, from left to right, consisted of (first row) Louis Belvail, "Monk" Taeuffer, and Louie Bacigalupi; (second row) Teddy Lynch, Louis Foppiano, and John Miller; (third row) Fred Huebner, Romeo Passalacqua, Will Neely, and Ernest Hughes.

Henry "Cotton" Williams, the standout first baseman (first row, far right), was a member of the 1933 Odd Fellows team. Other members included the hard-hitting Rollin McCord and pitcher Waldo Iversen. The team won the IOOF championship with a 3-2 win over Napa.

In the 1920s, Healdsburg's Prune Packers fielded a formidable semi-pro baseball team. Named after one of the town's cash crops, the Packers defeated the county opposition and went on to compete against Bay Area semipro teams. Large crowds of 800 and more people attended their home games at Recreation Park. The original Packers disbanded in the late 1920s, although the team was revived in the 1950s.

Competing with other semipro teams such as the Santa Rosa Rosebuds and the Petaluma Leghorns, the Healdsburg Prune Packers respectably represented their fruit-producing hometown. Many on the team, which was begun in 1928 and ended in the 1960s, were also prune pickers at some time in their lives in Healdsburg.

The 1906 Healdsburg High School football team, at and an average of 150 pounds, was one of the heaviest squads the school fielded up to that time. Among the team members on the squad were the McDonough brothers: Melville (middle row, second from left) and Bert and Lester (back row, second and third from left). Track star Fred Young is in the front row, left.

The first Healdsburg alumni football game was played on Thanksgiving Day 1928 and became an annual event interrupted only by World War II. The contest resumed in 1949 with profits from attendance going to the purchase of athletic equipment for the high school. Pictured are the 1957 Healdsburg Greyhounds scoring one of their two touchdowns in a 13-0 victory over the alumni team.

With "H"s emblazoned on their athletic shirts, the 1941 Healdsburg Grammar School boys' basketball team, assembles in front of the school entrance for a group photograph.

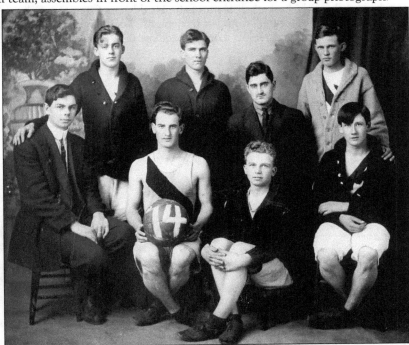

The Healdsburg High School Basketball team of 1914, though short in numbers, was tall in enthusiasm and ability. Pictured here are (first row) Ernest Frellson (manager), Claude Burke (center-captain), Glen Dewey (forward), and Elmer Sandborn (guard); (second row) Sewell Hilgerloh (forward), Albert Hoskinson (guard), Humbert Scatena (coach), and Alfred Parker (substitute).

In 1910, members of the girls' basketball team of the Healdsburg Grammar School line up in middy blouses and bloomers. Pictured, from left to right, are Lucile Byington, Marion Whitney, Jean Tevendale, Edna Haigh, Eda Beeson, Loraine McDonough, Claire Heald, Bernice Jaggers, Mildred Coffman, and Helen Hilgerloh.

The Healdsburg High School girls' basketball team of 1908 won the Academic Athletic League championship by defeating Cogswell Polytechnic College of Oakland by a score of 16-14. The determined-looking members, who lost only two games, from left to right, are Audrey Walters, Elva Beeson, Aubry Butler, Kathleen Swisher, Gertrude Field, Una Williams, and Bera Mothorn.

In 1910, Olympic champion Ralph Rose, third from right, and a star-studded assemblage of trackmen reconvened for an alumni track meet with Healdsburg High School athletes. The meet, organized by photographer and runner Mervyn Silberstein, second from right, actually ended in a tie score in points per team, but Rose did set a record in the 16-pound shot put.

Fred Young, vaulting for a remarkably talented Healdsburg High School team in 1909, went on to become a champion pole vaulter for the University of California, Berkeley. The high-flying Young later became a trusted undertaker in town.

In 1909, local hero and track legend Eddie Beeson shows his form in a record-breaking performance, at a meet in Berkeley for the University of California. Beeson's style of rolling over the bar, sometimes called the "Western Roll" was a precursor to the famous "Fosbury Flop" of the 1970s. This technique of leading with one's shoulders is now the standard in high jump competition.

Manuel Cordova, whose Pomo name was *Tuila* (Hummingbird), became a local marathon hero. Born in the Dry Creek Valley, the fleet-footed Native American was a participant in many long distance events, including the grueling 480-mile race from San Francisco to Grants Pass, Oregon, in 1928.

The "first lady of tennis," Hazel Hotchkiss Wightman was known for her aggressive, hard-pressing style of play that set the tone for future players to emulate. She was raised on a 375-acre family farm south of Healdsburg. Winning the Olympic gold medal in 1924, she was honored on this U.S. postage stamp in 1990.

Al Worden's Healdsburg High School championship tennis team of 1949 featured Stan Smith (top row center), who never lost a match in his four years as a Greyhound racquet man. Pictured here, from left to right, are (first row) E. Nicoletti, B. Mazetti, and J. Brooks; (second row) Worden, C. Wilson, Stan Smith, Alfred Elgin, and R. Pierce.

The proper handling of a rifle is demonstrated in 1957 by R. W. Peterson, instructor in Healdsburg's Junior Hunting Safety Course, on the grounds of the Healdsburg Rod and Gun Club. His class includes, from left to right, Dan Brewer, Dean Ross (behind), Joe Brewer, Seth Hartman, Robert Burg, Nathan Cox, and Ann Petray.

In this 1947 image, Ralph and Jake Tanner proudly display steelhead trout caught in the Russian River. The local hotspots produced many species of salmon for local sportsmen.

Eight

ABUNDANCE AND ENTERPRISE

The logging industry was a strong force in the local economy in the 19th century. Rich stands of redwood and other timber along the Russian River system fed the multiplying sawmills and lumberyards into the 20th century. Rumors of gold never panned out, but mercury, used in gold processing, was discovered in significant amounts in the mountainous region to the north. Little mining communities, which relied heavily on immigrant Chinese labor, sprang up to accommodate the influx of miners, but vanished in hard times. One mining enterprise, taking gravel from the Russian River aquifer for construction purposes, began at the turn of the 20th century and is still pursued.

Pioneer farmers found that the temperate climate and alluvial soil of the surrounding valleys created an agricultural paradise. The abundance of fruit called forth packinghouses and canneries in the late 19th century. It meant seasonal work for hundreds of local women and girls. Over the decades, grapes, hops, and prunes emerged as the chief money crops. The boom years for local hops—prized by brewers as a bitter flavoring agent—lasted from the 1880s to the 1950s. Local prunes also fell out of demand about the same time. At the height of production, blossoming prune trees created a sweeping springtime spectacle.

The mountainous area north of Healdsburg proved to be an important source of quicksilver, or sulphate of mercury, which was an essential element in the processing of pure gold and silver. From the 1800s and well into the 20th century, mines and small mining communities revived and expired depending on mercury prices. The Socrates Mine, 22 miles northeast of Healdsburg, crushed and concentrated the cinnabar ore in mountain-side processing plants.

Pioneers discovered rich stands of redwood along the Russian River system in the Healdsburg region. It was a resource that founded the first important industry. Felling a redwood was a daunting, day-long task, pitting a small team of workers with hand tools against a massive trunk, as demonstrated in this *c.* 1900 picture. Redwood lumber helped rebuild San Francisco after its several massive fires.

Teams of oxen hauled wagonloads of logs from the lumber camps along the Russian River and its tributaries in the 19th century. Redwood was the most sought-after lumber for building. During the Civil War, redwoods were cut and shipped to the North for use as railroad ties. The arrival of the railroad in Healdsburg in 1871 greatly expanded the markets for local lumber.

A. F. Stevens, owner of the A. F. Stevens Lumber Company, is the man in the suit in front of the wagonload of lumber. He bought the yard in 1908 and developed it into one of the town's most successful businesses. On his death in 1928, his son Russell took charge. The lumberyard is still in business as the Healdsburg Lumber Company.

The local abundance of tan oak trees, whose bark was used for curing leather, encouraged one of the town's earliest enterprises, the manufacture of leather gloves. This 1872 view shows the Healdsburg tannery of Gordon A. Cook, a native of New York State who came to Healdsburg in 1865 and turned from farmer to glove manufacturer around 1870.

The harvest season for bark from tan oak trees in northwest Sonoma County was in May and June. Workers, based in woodland camps, peeled the tannin-rich bark from the trees and hauled it out in sections to manufacturers. Mules pulled the wagons in the early years. The harvesting persisted into the 20th century. Here is a typically loaded motor truck, c. 1920.

In the 1870s, farmers in the fertile valleys around Healdsburg raised grain on much of their acreage in an era before crop specialization—grapes, hops, and prunes—became the mainstay of agriculture in the area. The Healdsburg Flouring Mill, sketched here in 1877, was located on the south side of town. A railroad engine, a certain sign of progress, steams past in the background.

This advertisement is from a March 1875 edition of the *Russian River Flag*, a Healdsburg weekly. T. C. Carruthers and his associates were regular advertisers in the newspaper, inviting local farmers to bring in their wagonloads of grain to be ground into flour.

In 1874, the shriek of steam released from the boiler valve of a threshing machine pierces a May day just south of the Plaza. The note on the back of the original image indicates Clarence Downing, the brother of the photographer, had just completed a repair of the machine and was returning it to work in the grain fields. He soon left town to become a successful mechanical engineer in San Francisco.

C. J. Aydt family members and workers made up a team of threshers who, in the late 19th century, moved from ranch to ranch helping to harvest the grain crops that were an important source of farm revenue in those days. The horse-drawn, cabin-on-wheels served as cookhouse and bunkhouse. Some workers slept underneath it. Harvest time provided an opportunity to advertise coal for the coming winter.

In the late 1880s, canneries and food packing plants began popping up in Healdsburg. The town shipped thousands of cases of fruit and vegetables to the East Coast and Midwest, as well as Europe and Australia. The work was seasonal and performed predominately by women, as demonstrated in this group photograph of the peach canning process at the Magnolia Cannery. The industry was important to the local economy and lasted well into the 20th century.

The wooden crates carrying canned fruits and vegetables in the 19th century bore identifying labels that developed into eye-catching artwork by the mid-1880s in California and other states. The Magnolia Fruit Company of Healdsburg advertised in 1888 that it would need to hire about 200 to 250 women, boys, and girls to work preparing and canning local fruit crops.

The Healdsburg Enterprise

HEALDSBURG, CALIFORNIA, SATURDAY, JANUARY 8, 1916

ONE HUNDRED AND FIFTY THOUSAND PRUNE TREES ARE BEING PLANTED

PRUNE INDUSTRY OF NORTHERN SONOMA GROWING BY MUCH PLANTING

Two Thousand Acres to Be Set Out Before Spring—Partial List of Those Setting Out Prune Trees—Steady Growth for Years

acres.
C. D. Masters, Alexander Valley, 11 acres.
Perry McPherson, Alexander Valley, 5 acres.
Bud McPherson, Alexander Valley, 8 acres.
A. L. McPherson, Alexander Valley, 6½ acres.
Sarah Kelley, West Side, 9 acres.

Demand for prunes from the Healdsburg region intensified with the outbreak of World War I in 1914. Local prunes were "known the world over for their excellent quality," according to the *Healdsburg Enterprise*. There was a rush to plant new prune orchards in 1916. In an age before widespread refrigeration, prunes were a welcome fruit dish in the winter and spring months. At the peak of prune plantings in California in 1929, some 171,330 acres, or 267.7 square miles, were planted in prune orchards.

One of the most delightful aspects of the prune-producing era in the Healdsburg area was the explosion of prune blossoms in the spring. This is a westerly view from Fitch Mountain overlooking the blossoming orchards of the Minaglia Ranch on Bailhache Avenue. The Russian River flows toward town in the foreground.

Trays of prunes are spread out for sun drying at the Hotchkiss Ranch on Eastside Road between Healdsburg and Windsor in about 1900. This was the family home of Hazel Hotchkiss Wightman, who became an Olympic tennis star. Both towns claim her as their hometown champ.

The sheer volume of prunes handled by Healdsburg's Sherriffs Brothers Packing House, one of the largest in Sonoma County, is demonstrated by this c. 1918 image of a worker maintaining banks of the dried fruit. During a bumper crop, about 5,000 tons of prunes went through the packinghouse in the south part of town near the railroad tracks. Sherriffs sold the business in 1922 to the California Prune and Apricot Growers.

Two young hop pickers strip vines at the Chisholm Hop Ranch. The long gloves provided protection from the irritating rough leaves and stems. The large hat shaded the woman from exposure to the late summer sun. It was hot sticky work, paying the pickers 1½¢ per pound in the 1930s.

During a typical harvest in the early years of the 20th century, whole families camped near the hop fields, and parents and children spent the day stripping the hops from the vines. Migrant workers joined the locals in the harvesting.

The Wohler Ranch hop kilns were among the many operating around Healdsburg in the early decades of the 20th century. Hop blossoms were stripped from the vines and taken to the kilns where they were dried and shipped to be used in the brewing of beer. Hops were first planted in the area in the 1870s. By the 1960s, they were no longer a commercial crop because of a fungal blight and a switch to lighter-tasting beer.

Driver Matt Hughes delivers a wagonload of hops to the Wohler Ranch hop kiln, c. 1910. In the harvest season, a stream of horse-drawn wagons delivered the crop to the drying kilns of the region. The dried hop blossoms were shipped to brewers who used them in the beer-making process to add a distinctively bitter flavor.

The departure of the first freight load of gravel for the building of the concrete foundations of the Golden Gate Bridge was a ceremonial moment for Healdsburg's Basalt Rock Company in 1935. Developer John D. Grant, right, was one of the first in the early 20th century to mine the deep gravel layers of the Russian River aquifer. It became an important local industry during the construction expansion after World War II.

The shovel and horse-drawn wagon of the early days of gravel mining have been replaced by the high-extraction equipment in this c. 1940 picture. The production method, mining by drag line, involves swinging the bucket into the Russian River and dragging it ashore holding about three cubic yards of sand and gravel. The load is emptied into a waiting "cat wagon." (Courtesy of Rand Dericco.)

Healdsburg developer John D. Grant optioned 2,500 acres in The Geysers canyon in 1920 and drilled a well, finding steam at 200 feet. He harnessed the steam for a power plant and began supplying Healdsburg with supplemental electricity. Contemporary equipment could not withstand the corrosive effects of steam, and it wasn't until the mid-1950s that large-scale power production was feasible in The Geysers field.

The geothermal energy of The Geysers was harnessed to provide electricity for the resort when entrepreneur John D. Grant, left, installed the first natural steam generator in America in 1923. Grant also established the first gravel grading plant in California on the Russian River in 1906.

YOU CAN'T
BEAT HEALDSBURG FOR

PRUNES, HOPS AND GRAPES

AND FOR
EVERYTHING THAT GROWS
UNDER THE SHINING SUN

CLIMATE, SCENERY, RESORTS, RIVER, FLOWERS,
BEAUTIFUL HOMES AND PRETTY GIRLS

VISIT
HEALDSBURG

Hispanic migrants also provided labor to harvest the diverse crops grown in the Healdsburg area. Pictured are members of the Moreno family weighing in a basket of string beans they have picked at the Baudau ranch. At left is Robert Jackson, a Santa Rosa Junior High School teacher, who worked as a field representative and weigh master at the ranch during the summer months.

This promotional item from early in the 20th century, believed to be an ink blotter, relies on a heavy play-on-words to deliver its message. The beet shape is a visual reference to the "You can't beat Healdsburg" theme.

Nine

GRAPES IN PROFUSION

The vibrant wine industry now established in the Healdsburg region has deep roots in the community. In 1862, the town's first winemaker was George Miller, a Swiss native who built his Sotoyome Winery north of the Plaza. In 1873, John Chambaud, a French immigrant, established a stone winery on the southeast side of town near the new railroad tracks. His first vintage, from grapes grown by others, amounted to 20,000 gallons. Two brothers from Tuscany, Giuseppe and Pietro Simi, bought the Chambaud winery and by the 1880s were producing from 40,000 to 70,000 gallons of wine annually for the San Francisco market. They outgrew the Chambaud winery. In 1890, they built a bigger stone winery on the road north of town. The Simi winery building is still in use today.

The early winemakers struggled. *Phylloxera*, a root-eating pest, attacked the vineyards late in the 19th century. Nothing worked against the infestation until growers grafted their European-bred vines to resistant root stock of native American vines.

Prohibition lasted from 1919 to 1933. In 1939, the market price for grapes was $16 a ton, about the same price that was paid in 1900. It wasn't until the 1970s that wine grapes began emerging as the dominant agricultural crop of the region. The heritage of these persevering growers and winemakers is all around us.

The hard labor involved in tending new vineyards without mechanized equipment is illustrated in this c. 1918 image of the Dry Creek Valley. Carlo and Vince Davini, twin brothers, have a horse and a hand pick to till the soil on their property off Lytton Springs Road which is beyond the barn on the right. The vineyard is believed to have been planted with red wine grapes, likely zinfandel.

Picking grapes was a family affair on the Simi vineyards, *c.* 1925. Isabelle Simi Haigh, daughter of a founder of the winery, and her daughter Vivien about 10 at the time, are together on the left of this picture. The Simi Winery made sacramental wine during Prohibition (1919–1933) and sold off parcels of property to survive. When Prohibition ended, Simi was said to have some of the finest bottling of aged Sonoma red wine.

Grapes on the vine in northern Sonoma County benefit from a climate that offers a growing season of hot, dry days tempered by cool nights.

Teams haul grapes from the Hopkins ranch on Westside Road to be crushed in Windsor, c. 1900. The driver in the foreground is Marshall McCracken. In 1930, the ranch was bought by Osborne and Alice Aileen White. The Episcopal Diocese of California took over the property in 1947 to use as a retreat. Now known as The Bishop's Ranch, the beautiful site has facilities available to the public by reservation.

The Scatena Brothers Winery, a large frame structure built in 1890 on Grove Street, receives a load of grapes from the Porter ranch on Westside Road (now the MacMurray ranch) during the c. 1910 crush. The winery survived Prohibition by making medicinal and sacramental wine. The property was sold in the 1940s and now is the location of the Seghesio Family Vineyards winery and tasting room. (Courtesy of the Gail Unzelman collection.)

The Oliveto Winery, with Domenico Lorenzini as principal owner, was active from 1898 to Prohibition in 1919. Here are redwood fermenting tanks around 1900. Some 2,000 tons of grapes from Sonoma, Mendocino, and Lake Counties were crushed annually and the wine sold from the Oliveto depot in San Francisco.

This Mervyn Silberstein photograph of the Simi Winery shows wine filtering equipment characteristic of the early 1900s. An old wine press is pictured in the center.

A man operates a bottle filler at Simi Winery, *c.* 1900. Wine bottles were filled largely by hand until automated bottling lines became common in the 1960s. In the 1970s and 1980s, with the increase in demand for fine wine, there were innovations in the California wine industry that advanced the efficiency of packaging systems and improved winemaking technology.

The stone building of the Simi Winery, still standing in north Healdsburg by the railroad tracks, was built in 1890 by Guiseppi and Pietro Simi, brothers who emigrated from their native Italy. They founded the winery in 1874, and became American citizens in the 1880s. Here, *c.* 1900, winery workers are loading barrels of wine from the winery dock into a railroad car.

The Paxton Winery building, erected in 1887, was designed by Hamden W. McIntyre, a leading winery architect of that era. McIntyre also designed many well-known Napa Valley wineries, including the Christian Brothers Winery and Inglenook Winery (now Niebaum-Coppola). The 1906 earthquake collapsed the four-foot-thick walls of the Paxton Winery and only a small portion of the stone work still stands. Wealthy John A. Paxton also built the mansion on Madrona Knoll, now known as Madrona Manor.

In 1881, immigrant Andrea Sbarboro conceived of the Italian Swiss Agriculture Colony as an investment property. Italian and Swiss families were invited to settle, farm, and invest in the land some 12 miles north of Healdsburg. They created the village of Asti. The Italian Swiss Colony winery, shown here c. 1947, produced award-winning wines and had a storage capacity of 10 million gallons.

Louis J. Foppiano stands on one of the railroad tank cars leased by the company in the late 1930s to ship bulk wine to New York for bottling. The tank cars were brought to a rail siding near the Foppiano winery, which still produces wine at the location southwest of Healdsburg. In the late 1930s, with the effect of Prohibition (1919–1933) still being felt, it was more economical to ship in bulk rather than bottle locally. (Courtesy of Louis J. Foppiano.)

A stream of red wine runs down a roadside ditch from the Foppiano ranch, southwest of Healdsburg. In 1926, Prohibition authorities ordered the dumping of the wine stocks on hand. A crowd, numbered at between 30 and 40 men and women by the local press, gathered to scoop up the wine "as one might scoop water from a babbling brook." (Courtesy of Louis J. Foppiano.)

Phil Ponzo Jr. of Dry Creek Valley stands before the Healdsburg Wine Producers store, which he and his father established around 1915 on Vallejo Street in San Francisco. It was a bold move for local vintners to market in the big city. Father and son report "a good demand for their wines," the *Healdsburg Enterprise* said. (Courtesy of Bunny Lewers.)

Isabelle Simi Haigh and her husband, Fred Haigh, enjoy a relaxing moment at a dining table complete with glasses of red wine, c. 1940s. Wine was served daily at dinner by families of Italian origin. It was hard for them to understand how a custom followed for centuries in the old country could be repressed in the United States during the Prohibition years.

An old redwood fermentation tank served as the tasting room for Simi Winery for many years. Beginning in 1904 when she inherited the winery, Isabelle Simi Haigh worked here selling wine and managing her winery. In the early days, the wine often was labeled Montepulciano after the Italian wine-growing area where the founding Simi brothers were born. The tank was used as the Simi tasting room until the mid-1970s, when the present tasting room was built.

Isabelle Simi Haigh and her husband, Fred Haigh, seated on the right, join in the hospitality of the tasting room within the redwood tank at Simi Winery in an image that appears to date from the 1950s. The wide array of wines on the tasting table includes an unopened bottle of champagne. A cork-opener is clamped to the table top on the right.

Fredrick Otto Brandt drives a decorated float, *c.* 1911, displaying the variety of products from Brandt's bottling firm. Even the horses were decorated for this Fourth of July parade. Brandt, a German immigrant, settled his family in Healdsburg in the late 1880s, and started a brewery.

During the late 1890s, F. O. Brandt's brewery on University Street between Matheson and North Streets began bottling beer from other breweries and manufacturing flavored cream sodas and seltzer water. Brandt promoted his company as "Healdsburg Soda and Bottling Works." By 1908, the manufacture of ice had become such an important function that the name of the company was changed to "Healdsburg Bottling and Ice Works."

Ten

CALAMITIES AND REJOICING

A farm town located by a temperamental river in earthquake country was destined to experience bad times. In the good times, the townsfolk loved a celebration. The Plaza and the river under the bridges were natural sites for elaborate, fanciful occasions involving a huge investment in time and attracting visitors from around the county. One annual tradition in the 19th century was for men to put on knights' costumes and try to lance wooden rings from horseback. At the turn of the century, floral parades around town and water carnivals on the river were ruled over by young women elevated to ceremonial queens with full courts. Community spirit also went into good causes; the town "adopted" a U.S. Army battalion in the Korean War.

On the down side, the great earthquake of 1906 destroyed a three-story building on Healdsburg's Plaza and damaged other structures. There were concerns every winter about the Russian River overflowing its banks after heavy rainstorms. One of the worst floods, in 1937, inundated hundreds of acres of crop land and resort property. The Depression in the 1930s weighed heavily on the town despite morale-building attempts. Some of the unemployed found temporary jobs with the Works Progress Administration (WPA).

Mabelle Shelford and Florence Barnes pose in a flower-decorated rig under a pretty parasol in preparation for the 1904 Floral Festival parade.

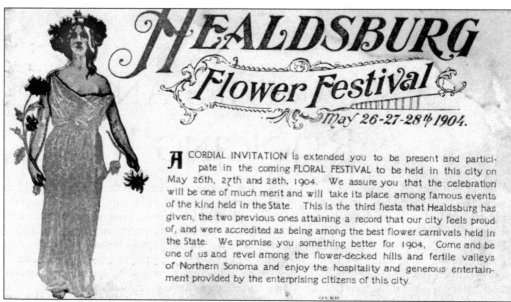

This postcard-sized invitation promised Healdsburg's third flower festival in 1904 would be better than the previous two, and "those were accredited as being among the best . . . in the State." The other side featured Healdsburg's city hall—"the finest in the county"—and noted the Plaza was adorned "with streamers of electric lights from the four corners."

A formal portrait of the queen of the 1909 Water Carnival and her court in full regalia shows how seriously Healdsburg took the coronation. Queen Stella Lufkin was described in the local press as "one of Healdsburg's most charming belles."

"Queen Flora" Isabelle Simi reigned over the 1904 Floral Festival. A few months following the festival, her father died and the teenaged Isabelle took over the operation of the Simi Winery. The winery is still in operation in Healdsburg today.

Alice Haigh, the 1896 Floral Festival Queen, and her regally attired court ladies and small attendants gather for a formal portrait. Standing, from left to right, they are (first row) Zoe Bates, Bert McDonough, princess Julie Mehrtens, queen Alice Haigh, Van Whitney, and Nettie Barnes; (second row) Violet Luedke, Edna Biddle, Nellie Petray, and Lena Zane.

Healdsburg's 1896 Floral Festival featured a popular parade of decorated carriages and bikes and the coronation of a festival queen. Two other festivals were held with equally great success in 1895 and 1904.

Queen Emma Meiler of the 1895 Floral Festival and her court make the royal circuit of the Plaza lined with spectators. Behind the carriage, the Union Hotel, decked with bunting, offered choice viewing seats on the second-story veranda. The floral festivals at the turn of the century evolved from May Day celebrations in the 1870s. The coronation of the queen in 1895 opened a three-day celebration.

The royal barge passes under the railroad bridge in a procession of decorated floats on the Russian River during the 1909 Water Carnival. The celebration was first held in 1905 and included diving exhibitions from the bridge and fireworks at night.

Pictured *c.* 1895, Mounted knights escorted the Floral Queen's royal carriage to the Plaza and later participated in the tilting tournament. Two teams of five men each attempted to spear the rings hung under arches on Center Street.

Store owners, smithies, barkeeps, and other townsmen assembled in costume *c.* 1877 for the annual May Day Festival and Knighthood Tournament, first held in Healdsburg in 1857, the year the town was founded. The "knights for the day" tried to catch wooden rings with the point of a seven-foot lance while galloping on a horse.

In 1910, the Pastime Minstrels and the Healdsburg Town Band assemble in front of the highly popular Truitt's Opera House on Center Street. As early as 1888, Truitt's theater was featuring social dances, dramas, musical concerts, and lectures. In 1891, the Healdsburg Minstrels gave their first performance there. Roland Truitt, a showman himself, is in the center of the second row of this picture, behind the band master.

The Sotoyome Band was formed in the 1880s, and played at the dedication of the first Healdsburg City Hall in 1886. Although the band had only 15 members, they played a full program of marches, waltzes, and other selections. The popular band delighted crowds through the early 1900s at their Saturday night open-air concerts in the Plaza.

In 1924, the Healdsburg Chamber of Commerce held a slogan contest to promote its importance as a prune-growing center. The contest was widely publicized and there were more than 2,500 entries competing for the $100 prize for the best 10-words-or-less slogan. The winner, "Healdsburg: the Buckle of the Prune Belt," is displayed on this c. 1930s float carrying a bowl of paper mache prunes. The young woman standing on the right is Elsie Nardi. (Courtesy of Francis Passalacqua.)

Reversing the order of things in the usual Squeedunk manner, a white mule pushes along a carriage equipped with a giant navigation wheel. An amused crowd lines the Plaza as the vehicle occupied by Ted Garrett and Donald Brown passes in a c. 1927 Squeedunk parade. The Squeedunks originally were formed in 1876 in reaction to the patriotic outpouring of the centennial year.

114

In the mid-1950s, the Rose Parade through downtown Santa Rosa gave Healdsburg a chance to show off the tourist advantage of having the Russian River at its doorstep. The young women being towed by the Healdsburg Boat Club were promoting a forthcoming Fourth of July celebration on water. During the summer, the club organized boating picnics on the river every Wednesday evening.

A bucking automobile is a typical feature of a Squeedunk parade, c. 1920s, during a revival of the antic group activities in Healdsburg. The Squeedunks were formed in 1876 in a humorous reaction to the outpouring of the centennial year patriotism. For about 40 years, they followed community parades on the Fourth of July with their own burlesque procession.

A cast of some 70 men, half of them impersonating women, presented two performances of "When Men Marry" in the American Legion Hall in April 1936. Prominent citizens of the town, the *Healdsburg Tribune* said, "cast aside their somber business suits" to play matrons, vamps, and

fashion plates. The production, a benefit for a youth baseball team, involved high society antics, but the *Tribune* admitted it "didn't have much of a plot."

The 1906 earthquake destroyed the three-story Odd Fellows Hall at West (now Healdsburg Avenue) and Matheson Streets. It was the worst damage in town and the single largest loss at $15,000. Next to it on the left, the Cohen Building, which housed a furniture business, was flattened.

Whitney's Pharmacy on Center Street sustained major damage in the 1906 earthquake when the falling walls of the Masonic Building crushed its roof. Despite pharmacist Whitney's $6,000 loss in the disaster, he set up and sold his remaining merchandise in the bowling alley.

Will Cummings guides his four-horse team across the Russian River on his way up to the Socrates quicksilver mine with a load of supplies. He forded the river because the Alexander Valley bridge was destroyed in the 1906 earthquake.

The flooding of the Russian River in December 1937 inundated hundreds of acres of farm and resort land and threatened the two bridges at Healdsburg. This image looks south at the Redwood Highway bridge.

In this image of the 1937 flooding, the water surges up to the superstructure of the railroad bridge. During a later flood, rail cars filled with gravel were left on the bridge to help hold it in place, lest the raging waters sweep it away.

On April 20, 1933, Healdsburg tried to lift the spirits of the community by holding a funeral for "Old Man Depression" and taking the casket in a procession to the railroad station. Waiting was a promotional freight train loaded with redwood lumber to be distributed to yards throughout the Redwood Empire in anticipation of a building boom. The casket was loaded aboard the train. The Depression continued.

The Works Progress Administration (WPA), which put to work millions of unemployed men during the Depression, provided labor for public improvement projects in Healdsburg. The A. F. Stevens Lumber Company was part of the effort. Here Russell Stevens, son of the company founder, left, and a colleague lean on shovels in the classic pose of WPA workers taking a break. Critics of the program thought there were too many breaks.

On November 11, 1918, a spontaneous Armistice Day parade rolls around the Plaza. The lead automobile carries Mayor George Brigham Jr., with the Stars and Stripes, and town poet Julius M. Alexander with the flag of peace he designed for a newspaper contest. The face masks were a precaution against the influenza pandemic which began in World War I and caused deaths in Healdsburg.

JAIL REGISTER

A. CARLISLE & CO., STATIONERS & PRINTERS, N.Y. 20606

UMBER	NAME	DATE RECEIVED	ACCOMPANYING OFFICER	CHARGE		Sex	Age	RACE	PLACE OF BIRTH
08	Phill Gilbried	Oct 22	W Studer	Drunk		male	44	amer	Healdsbug
09	Rich Sealira	" 24	mcbod	Speeding		"	19	Ital	S X
10	Rodger Gilbried	" 30	S ruebod	Drunk		"	44	amer	Healdsbug
11	J H Otcany	" 30	S ruebd	"	"	"	40	Irish	Illinois
12	Jos Sinclair	" 30	mason + Stu	Beg		m	64	am	-
13	John Cook	Nov 6	mason	Drunk		m	57	amer	Xo Berg
14	Dan Kosler	" 6	mason	Petit Larceny		m	21	"	-
15	James Oconor	" 9	mc o Stu	No mask + Drunk		m	51	Irish	-
16	Geo Watterman	" 9	Clyde	Not Wear mask		m	61	amer	Petaluma
17	Arthur Edwards	" 9	Clyde	" "		m	41	"	-
18	Waller Scott	" 9	Clyde	" "		m	47	"	Xo Berg
19	Wm Miller	" 9	Clyde	" "		m	48	"	" "
20	W. R Paget	" 9	Clyde	" "		m	-	"	" "

The city jail register for November 1918 shows the desperate measures Healdsburg was taking to defend against the deadly influenza pandemic. Town leaders made it an offense for residents to appear in public without an approved face mask. The first arrest on the charge was November 9 and many others followed. The law remained on the books for two months before health authorities said it was safe to remove the masks.

Victory gardens were patriotic demonstrations in World War I as well as in World War II. The idea was to help produce food for home consumption and lessen the demand on the farmers involved in the war effort. The Healdsburg Grammar School provided this example, *c.* 1918, of boys in town clothes displaying farming skills on the school grounds.

Healdsburg native son Julius Myron Alexander, a descendant of pioneer Cyrus Alexander, is pictured with the banner he designed to promote world peace, prior to the outbreak of World War I. In September 1914, the *Healdsburg Tribune* described "a monster peace gathering" in San Francisco's Golden Gate Park at which his Peace Flag was first unfurled. Sixteen young ladies, in costumes of different nations, marched behind Miss Liberty bearing the Peace Flag. At the peak of the ceremony, they each released a single white dove, while the Peace Flag was waved in front of a crowd of 100,000 people singing "The Star-Spangled Banner."

In 1943, during World War II, the elementary schoolchildren of Healdsburg led a bond drive to "buy" a military aircraft. The goal was $75,000 worth of bonds, but with enthusiastic community support, the final pledge came to $105,000. As a symbolic reward, a P-47 Thunderbolt fighter was christened the *City of Healdsburg.* After a successful war bonds tour of America, the plane went to England and the 8th Air Force, assigned to the 352nd Fighter Group.

In 1954, Civil Defense Ground Observer Corps volunteers received a new acoustic detector. Robert Mascherini, far right, shows the device, one of five in California, to observers at the Tayman Park post. Observers pictured, from left to right, are Mrs. Charles Scalione, Mrs. Waldo Iversen, Mrs. W. A. Archer, Mrs. Mel Wood, and W. A. Archer.

Healdsburg adopted the First Battalion of the U. S. Army's 7th Infantry Regiment in 1951 during the Korean War after the commander, Lt. Col. Fred Weyand, wrote his wife in Healdsburg about the scarcity of non-military items. Spearheaded by Smith Robinson, here seated right, the town's campaign produced a first shipment of tinned snacks, washcloths, combs, mirrors, sewing kits, stationery, and Brownie cameras. Citizens gathered together to bake cookies and prepare packages for the battalion. Also included were the addresses of local girls who would correspond.

Packages shipped from Healdsburg arrived in time for Christmas 1952 distribution to members of the First Battalion, 7th Infantry Regiment. Here Cpl. Vernon Wilmer, left, of Baltimore, and M. Sgt. George T. Petty, of Scottsville, Kentucky, look over part of that 42-package shipment. Healdsburg's "adopted" battalion could look forward to another shipment of packages at Easter, thanks to Smith "Smitty" Robinson and Healdsburg citizens.

SURNAME INDEX

Albertson 56
Alexander 17, 19, 20, 63, 122, 123
Archer 124
Arnold 15
Athey 57
Auradou 59
Aydt 88
Babcock 72
Bacigalupi 74
Badger 59
Barnes 107, 110
Bates 110
Baudau 96
Beeson 37, 71, 78, 80
Belvail 74
Bennett 60
Biddle 110
Boehm 71
Bostwick 52
Bourne 45
Boyce 31
Brandt 106
Brewer 82
Brigham 122
Brooks 81
Brown 114
Burg 82
Burke 77
Bush 25, 29
Butler 78
Byington 27, 78
Carnegie 36
Carrillo 7, 18
Carroll 60
Carruthers 87

Chambaud 97
Chisholm 92
Coffman 78
Cohen 118
Cook 30, 86
Coolidge 45
Copa 14
Coppola 102
Cordova 15, 80
Cox 82
Cummings 31, 119
Davini 97
Day 35
Dewey 77
Dickson 69
Dollar 14, 15
Downing 29, 88
Elgin 15, 81
Elliott 50
Emerson 37, 52
Field 78
Fitch 7, 17-21
Foppiano 74, 103
Foss 51–53
Freas 14
Frellson 77
Gambetta 59
Garrett 30, 114
Gilliland 62
Gobbi 30, 72
Goldstein 74
Goodyear 31
Grant 19, 41, 49, 94, 95
Gray 27
Griest 37
Haigh 78, 98, 104, 105, 110

Haley 60
Hall 57
Hartman 82
Heald 7, 17, 22, 24, 63, 78
Hilgerloh 77, 78
Hopkins 99
Hoskinson 77
Hotchkiss 71, 81, 91
Huebner 74
Hughes 74, 93
Isaacson 69
Iversen 74, 124
Jackson 96
Jaggers 78
Johns 51
Johnson 69
Jones 36, 69
Kent 67
Kron 60
Langhart 16, 63
Lattin 53
LeBaron 35
Lewering 69
Lewis 60
Logan 37
Lorenzini 100
Lozinto 15, 16
Lucas 15
Lucero 17
Luedke 110
Lufkin 108
Lynch 74
MacMurray 99
Manuel 13
Marion 68
Mascherini 124

Matheson 17, 23, 30
Mazetti 81
McCord 74
McCracken 99
McDonough 76, 78, 110
McIntyre 102
McMullin 37
Mehrtens 110
Meiler 111
Micheletti 59
Miller 74, 97
Minaglia 90
Moore 49
Moreno 96
Mothorn 78
Nardi 114
Neely 74
Nicoletti 81
Niebaum 102
Norton 25, 28, 57
Paige 60
Parker 77
Passalacqua 74
Passarino 59
Patterson 60
Paxton 102
Peña 41
Peterson 82
Petray 37, 82, 110
Petty 125
Phillips 21, 37
Pierce 81
Piña 21
Ponzo 104
Porter 99
Powell 49

Rafanelli 59
Reynolds 37
Roberts 68
Robinson 70, 125
Rolph 45
Rose 71, 79
Rosenberg 25, 29
Ross 37, 82
Sandborn 77
Sbarboro 102
Sbragia 61
Scalione 124
Scatena 77, 99
Schieffer 43
Seaman 23
Seghesio 99
Seipel 34
Shaw 22, 37
Shelford 107
Sherriffs 91
Silberstein 2, 15, 79, 100
Simi 97, 98, 100, 101,
    104, 105, 109
Simpson 46, 68
Smith 16, 81
Snook 62
Solem 69
Somersal 12
Stevens 85, 121
Sullivan 37
Swisher 78
Taeuffer 74
Tanner 82
Tevendale 78
Thomson 39
Truitt 37, 113

Vercelli 60
Wagele 73
Wagner 69
Waho 15
Walters 78
Wetzel 20
Weyand 125
White 64, 65, 99
Whitney 78, 110, 118
Wightman 71, 81, 91
Williams 74, 78
Wills 71
Wilmer 125
Wilson 81
Wohler 93
Wolking 60
Wood 124
Worden 81
Young 25, 31, 76, 79
Zane 110

The Healdsburg Museum was founded in 1976 by a group of local citizens led by retired city clerk Edwin Langhart to house historical collections donated to the city. In 1990, the museum moved to its present quarters in the city's Carnegie Library building, dating from 1911. In 1994, the Healdsburg Museum and Historical Society combined to fund and operate the museum. Today the museum, operated by a paid staff and a large contingent of volunteers, is open to the public six days a week. (Courtesy of Daniel F. Murley.)

Visit the museum at 221 Matheson Street, Healdsburg, California

Contact the museum by mail at P.O. Box 952, Healdsburg, California, 95448 or by e-mail at healdsburgmuseum@sbcglobal.net.

Visit the website at www.healdsburgmuseum.org.

History Lives at the Healdsburg Museum.